52 PRAYERS FOR MY FUTURE HUSBAND

TYNDALE
MOMENTUM™

A Tyndale nonfiction imprint

52 PRAYERS

FOR MY

Future HUSBAND

— A DEVOTIONAL —

STEFANIE
ROUSE

Visit Tyndale online at tyndale.com.

52 Prayers for My Future Husband: A Devotional

Published in association with The Bindery Agency, www.TheBinderyAgency.com.

Cover design by Ellery Sterling

Interior design by Laura Cruise

Edited by Sarah Kelley

For information about special discounts for bulk purchases, please contact Tyndale House Publishers at csresponse@tyndale.com, or call 1-855-277-9400.

ISBN 979-8-4005-2330-4

Printed in China

32 31 30 29 28 27 26
7 6 5 4 3 2 1

To the love of my life, Caleb:

You are my walking redemption story and answer to prayer.

To Laura, Deanna, Sarah, Michelle, Mirta, Kristi, Brenda, Senam, Makayla, Alisa, Elisabeth, Katarina, and all our beloved community:

It's been the joy and honor of my life to walk beside you as you honor God in the way you live out singleness, dating, and marriage. Thanks for letting me walk beside you.

Introduction

Dear beloved reader,

If you've picked up this book, my guess is you have a longing in your heart. A longing for love. A longing for partnership. A longing to build a marriage that is rooted in faith and reflects the love of Christ.

Maybe you're single, desiring to faithfully pray for the man you haven't met yet. Maybe you're dating and wondering if this is the person God has chosen for you. Maybe you're engaged, preparing for one of the biggest seasons of your life with both excitement and nerves. Or maybe you've walked through heartbreak, divorce, or disappointment, and you wonder if God can redeem your story and still bring you a marriage that honors Him.

Wherever you are on your journey, this book is for you. As women, many of us grow up with a deep hope that one day we will meet and marry the love of our life. Maybe you've dreamed of your wedding day since you were little, picturing the dress, the flowers, and the moment you lock eyes with your future husband. Or maybe you've carried wounds from broken relationships or divorce that make you wonder if real love is still possible for you. You may be in a season of waiting, wondering when God's plan will unfold, or you may be dating or engaged, wanting to build a foundation for your relationship that is rooted in faith.

No matter where you find yourself on this journey, this devotional is for you. It's a powerful reminder that God sees you, loves you, and is writing a story far greater than you can imagine. My prayer is that these words will guide you not only to pray for your future husband but also to grow into the woman God has called you to be right now.

God Sees You

I want to begin with this truth: God sees you. He sees your tears, your prayers, and your longings. He knows the deepest desires of your heart. And He is not ignoring you. He is working, even when you can't see it. He is writing a beautiful story just for you.

I know what it feels like to wonder if God has forgotten about you. I know the ache of heartbreak, the heaviness of disappointment, and the questions that keep you awake at night: *Will I ever meet him? Am I too late? Did I mess things up?*

There were seasons in my own life when I felt unseen, when I thought love had passed me by. I walked through heartbreaks that left me questioning if marriage was really possible for me. Looking back, I can see God's fingerprints in every season. Even in the pain, He was shaping me. Even in the waiting, He was preparing me. And in His perfect timing, He brought my husband, Caleb, the love of my life and my partner in ministry, into my life.

Had I rushed ahead of God or clung to the wrong relationships, I would have missed His best. But through prayer, surrender, and patience, God gave me not only a husband but also a love story that reflects His goodness and grace.

Why Pray for Your Future Husband?

If you're single, maybe you've asked yourself, *What's the point of praying for someone I haven't even met yet?*

The answer is this: Prayer is not only about changing someone else's circumstances, but it's also about allowing God to transform your own heart. When you pray for your future husband, you're asking God to prepare him and you. You're inviting Him to align your desires with His, to heal the broken places in your heart, and to grow you into the woman He created you to be.

Prayer is not passive. It's powerful. Every time you pray, you're planting seeds into the soil of your future. You may not see the fruit immediately, but trust that God is cultivating something beautiful beneath the surface.

And here's the best part: Prayer draws you closer to Jesus. It reminds you that your ultimate hope isn't in marriage. It's in Christ. A husband can be a blessing, but he cannot complete you. Only Jesus can do that. The more you fall in love with Him, the more ready you will be to love your husband one day with grace, compassion, and strength.

Lastly, prayer is powerful. God hears our prayers. God sees your future husband right now. He knows the pain he's walking through. The trials, the questions he's holding in his heart. It's vital that you intercede for him.

How to Use This Devotional

This book is designed to be your companion as you walk through this season of life, whether your journey lasts a few months or many years. Each devotional is written with one specific focus for prayer and reflection, so you don't have to feel overwhelmed about where to start. Here's what you can expect in each devotion:

- **Scripture**
  At the top of the page, you'll find a passage from God's Word that connects to the week's theme. God's Word is alive and powerful. It's what sustains us when doubts creep in or when the waiting feels long. I encourage you to read the Scripture slowly, pray over it, and even commit it to memory. Let it anchor your heart in truth.
- **A Devotion**
  You'll then find a short story or reflection, sometimes from my own journey, sometimes from lessons God has taught me, that connects to the topic. These are meant to remind you that you're not alone in your struggles and to encourage you with real-life examples of God's faithfulness.
- **Prayer**
  After the reflection, you'll find a prayer written specifically for your future husband and your own heart. You can pray these words as they are or use them as a springboard for your own prayers. Don't worry about getting the

words right; God delights in hearing your heart, whether your prayer is messy, short, or beautifully eloquent.

- **Love in Action**
  Prayer isn't meant to stay on the page. That's why each devotional ends with a simple, practical step you can take to live out what you're praying. Sometimes it might be something you do for yourself, like journaling or practicing gratitude. Other times, it might be an action that blesses others, such as encouraging a friend, volunteering, or practicing forgiveness. Think of these steps as small seeds of love you're planting now that will one day bear fruit in your marriage.
- **Encouragement**
  Finally, you'll find a short word of encouragement to carry with you into the week. You may want to write it on a sticky note and place it where you'll see it daily, as a reminder of what God is doing in your life.

One way you can use this book is to focus on one devotion per week. That gives you the space to really let the Scripture sink in. You can even memorize the week's Scripture passage if you'd like, pray the same prayer each day for that whole week, and take time to live out the "Love in Action" step. When you linger with one devotional for seven days, you'll start to notice God weaving those truths into your daily rhythms.

The beauty of this book is that it isn't about speed but about letting God meet you right where you are and shape your heart through prayer.

The Heart Behind This Book

Friend, I want you to know that this devotional is not about striving to earn a husband or rushing God's timeline. It's about walking with Him day by day, trusting that His timing is perfect and letting Him shape your heart in the waiting.

Marriage is a beautiful gift, but it's not the ultimate prize. Jesus is. My prayer is that as you work through these pages, you will fall deeper in love with Him. Because when you are secure in His love, you'll be ready to love your husband from a place of wholeness rather than need.

A Blessing for You

As you begin this journey, I want to give you a blessing:

> May this devotional be a safe space where you bring your longings, your heartbreaks, and your hopes to God. May each prayer remind you that you are chosen, loved, and seen by Him. May you grow in compassion, patience, and grace, qualities that will bless not only your marriage one day but also every relationship in your life.
>
> And may you trust, with all your heart, that God's timing is perfect. He knows how to bring the right man into your life at the right time, and He knows how to prepare you to be the kind of wife who reflects His love.

A Prayer for You

Heavenly Father, *I lift up this beloved daughter of Yours who is holding this book in her hands right now. Thank You that You see her fully—every hope, every tear, every question, every dream. You know the longings of her heart for marriage, and You care deeply about them.*

Lord, I pray that as she walks through these pages, she would encounter Your presence in a fresh and powerful way. Remind her that she is chosen, treasured, and deeply loved by You. Where there has been heartbreak in her life, bring healing. Where there has been disappointment, bring fresh hope. Where there has been fear or doubt, replace it with trust in Your perfect timing.

Prepare her heart to love like You love. Grow in her compassion, patience, and strength. Shape her into the woman You have created her to be so that one day she may be a blessing to her future husband and a reflection of Christ in their marriage.

But more than anything, Lord, I ask that she would fall more in love with You through this journey. Let her find her security, joy, and identity in You alone. May her waiting not feel wasted but instead be a season of deep growth and intimacy with You.

Bless her future marriage, her future husband, and the love story You are writing. And bless her today, right where she is, as You are at work in her life in ways she cannot yet see. In Jesus' name, amen.

Your waiting is not wasted. Your prayers are not wasted. And your story is not over.

With much love and many blessings,

Stefanie Rouse
Christian relationship mentor

WEEK

1

GOD'S PLANS ARE BETTER THAN MINE

Now all glory to God, who is able, through his mighty power at work within us, to accomplish infinitely more than we might ask or think.

EPHESIANS 3:20

It was late and dark, and I was running along the golf course at Penn State University just hours after my engagement had ended. My heart was pounding hard, more from grief than from the distance I had run. I stumbled into an open bathroom, taking a seat on the cold bench, and stared at myself in the mirror as tears streamed down my face.

Just months before, my fiancé had slipped a ring on my finger and asked me to marry him. But now here I was—broken—asking God, *How could this be over? Isn't this the man You had planned for me?* I had been sure of it. While we were dating, I had fumbled through old journals to find the wish list I had for my future husband. He had seemed to check all the boxes. But now God was showing me something I couldn't see before. My list wasn't His list. Trivial things like his last name starting with *S* or his family living five minutes from mine weren't what really mattered. God was whispering to me in the midst of my confusion, "Your dreams are too small, but Mine are not."

I couldn't see my husband, Caleb, on the other side of my heartbreak just yet. I couldn't see the bigger story God was still writing. But that night on the golf course, God began loosening my grip on my plans so I could take hold of His.

Maybe you've been holding tightly to your own list or timeline. What if those dreams are too small? What if surrendering them to God is the very thing that will open your hands to His infinitely more?

Dear heavenly Father, *thank You for being a God whose plans are always better than mine. You see every dream I've had for my future marriage, every list I've made, and every prayer I've whispered. Today I lay those dreams before You, trusting that You know what is best.*

I lift up my future husband to You. Wherever he is right now, I ask that You give him clarity and peace about his own future. Protect him from chasing after things that won't last, and guard his heart from discouragement. Remind him that You are writing his story, too, and that Your timing is always perfect. Lord, grow him into a man who loves You more than anything else. Surround him with godly friends and mentors who will sharpen him. Shape his character so that he becomes a man of integrity, faith, and courage. Teach him to pray bold prayers, to walk in obedience, and to trust Your voice above all others.

Keep my heart from settling as well, Lord. Teach me to rest in You and to hope in Your promises. Thank You that You are weaving together a love story for me that reflects Your goodness. I trust that Your plans for my marriage are far better than anything I could imagine. In Jesus' name, amen.

Love in Action . . .

Take five minutes to write down one dream about your future marriage that you've been holding on to. Then pray over it, surrender it to God, and ask Him to shape it into His perfect plan.

God's plans for my marriage are better than anything I could imagine.

WEEK

2

GRACE IN OUR WEAKNESS

My grace is sufficient for you,
for my power is made perfect in weakness.
2 CORINTHIANS 12:9, NIV

I felt like everything was unraveling after my engagement ended. Friends had bought bridesmaid dresses they couldn't use, deposits were lost, and I was ashamed of letting so many people down. On top of it all, my senior year at Penn State was the hardest of my life. I had always been a diligent student, never missing class and always staying on top of my assignments. But in that season, I could barely keep track of what I had turned in. One day, I went up to a professor, apologizing for a late paper. I stumbled over my words, embarrassed that I wasn't the reliable student she was used to seeing.

I had been taught compassion throughout my life, but in that moment, I experienced grace and compassion from my professor like never before. Her grace for my weakness enlarged my heart. It opened my eyes to see that everyone is carrying battles whether they are visible or not. It helped me look for the best in people instead of assuming the worst. That hard season taught me more about grace—how I can receive it from God and how I can extend it to others as well.

Friend, sometimes our weakness becomes the very place where we realize how much we need God. It's not the end of us.

It's the beginning of seeing His strength in a whole new way. Whatever heartache you've walked through, let it not define you but refine you. Jesus wants to walk with you in it and help you find your way forward.

Lord, *thank You that Your grace is enough for us in every season. Thank You for the ways You've met me with compassion and for the people who have extended grace when I needed it most. I pray for my future husband, that he would know the power of Your grace in his own struggles and learn to walk in freedom instead of shame. I pray that he wouldn't view weakness the way the world does. Instead, let him see it as a way to trust You even more. Let all his pain and heartache push him to his knees and toward Your throne.*

And Lord, teach me to be a wife who will extend grace to him generously, not holding his weaknesses against him but building him up in love. Help me see my weakness as a way to rely on You even more.

I pray over our future marriage, that it would be a place marked by compassion, where Your grace flows freely between us and draws us closer to You. In Jesus' name, amen.

Love in Action . . .

Write down one weakness or shortcoming that has caused you to feel shame. Then ask God to use that very place to refine your character, increase your compassion, and prepare you to love your future spouse with grace.

My weakness doesn't define me. It refines me into someone ready to love with greater grace.

WEEK

3

TRUSTING GOD EVEN WHEN YOU FEEL FORGOTTEN

What is the price of five sparrows—two copper coins? Yet God does not forget a single one of them. And the very hairs on your head are all numbered. So don't be afraid; you are more valuable to God than a whole flock of sparrows.

LUKE 12:6-7

Where would I live? That was the question echoing in my heart after my engagement ended. Just months before, my life had been mapped out in my mind. I'd graduate from Penn State, move into my fiancé's condo, and work for the ministry he led. But now? Everything had vanished in an instant.

I remember walking across campus, feeling invisible, forgotten, and directionless. The enemy whispered, "See? No one is choosing you. Not even God." I cried out, "Lord, do You see me? Do You even care where I go from here?"

Then God surprised me with His kindness. I went on a mission trip with a new ministry and met the sweetest Christian woman, who welcomed me like family. She introduced me to another girl my age who just so happened to need a roommate. That opened the door to a house full of Christian women in ministry and a community that carried me and reminded me that God always sees me. Even when I felt forgotten, He was writing a better plan.

Dear one, whatever part of your story feels lost or overlooked, hold on to this: The God who carved your name into His nail-scarred hands has not forgotten you. He never will. In the unknown and uncertain times in life, He is the God who invites you to know Him. He is writing a story for your life that is better than you could imagine.

Dear heavenly Father, *thank You for being the God who never forgets. Thank You, Jesus, for carrying the cross, taking my sins, and engraving my name on Your hands. When I feel unseen, help me to picture Your nail-scarred hands holding mine.*

I pray over my future husband today. Remind him that he is not forgotten, not overlooked, not left behind. Protect him from lies of rejection and surround him with Your presence when he feels alone.

Show us both that You are making a way even in the wilderness, that You turn broken pieces into a masterpiece. Strengthen our trust in You as we wait for Your timing. In Jesus' mighty name, amen.

Love in Action . . .

Write Isaiah 49:16, "See, I have engraved you on the palms of my hands" (NIV), on a sticky note or in your journal. Whenever you feel overlooked, read it aloud and remind yourself that God has never forgotten you.

**Even when I feel unseen,
God never forgets me.**

WEEK

4

WAITING WITHOUT WASTING THE SEASON

Let's not get tired of doing what is good. At just the right time we will reap a harvest of blessing if we don't give up.

GALATIANS 6:9

There was a season when I had to face an uncomfortable truth: I wasn't as ready for marriage as I had once thought. I had been dumped by my fiancé three months before our wedding, and my newly single self was not thriving in the love department. I didn't know how to communicate my feelings in a way that built connection. I didn't know how to set boundaries. And deep down, I realized I was addicted to the approval of men.

This showed up in messy ways—saying yes to dates I knew were not God's best and constantly feeling like I had to earn love from others. Every setback or breakup left me not only more heartbroken but also questioning my worth. Maybe you've felt it, too, that ache of wondering if you'll ever "get it right."

But God is so kind. He didn't leave me in that desolate place. Instead of letting me continue in the same unhealthy patterns, He invited me to grow. For me, that meant counseling, inner-healing prayer, and mentors who spoke truth into my blind spots. It wasn't easy; growth never is. But slowly, the pieces of my heart started to come back together. I wasn't just waiting anymore; I was being prepared.

Looking back, I can see that what felt like wasted years was actually time God used to make me whole. God used the waiting season to teach me how to be healthy, how to find my worth in Him, and how to love in a way that lasts.

Maybe you feel like you're in that season now, wondering if you'll ever get where you want to be. Friend, take heart. The waiting isn't wasted when you let God use it to prepare you. This is not just the in-between. This is training ground.

Dear God, *thank You that You never leave us stuck. You always invite us to grow. I lift up my future husband to You today. Keep shaping him into the man You've called him to be. Give him courage to face the areas where he feels weak or unprepared and surround him with people who push him closer to You. Let him choose growth, healing, and wholeness, even in the waiting.*

You know the places I still need Your refining, Lord. Help me not to run from the hard work of growth but to press into it. When I feel tempted to compare or to coast, remind me that this season is a gift, a time where You're strengthening me to be the woman my future husband will one day need.

I pray for our future marriage. May it be built on two people who have said yes to growing in You first. Teach us to keep learning, keep listening, and keep becoming more like Jesus together. Let our story show the world that waiting on You is worth it. In Jesus' name, amen.

Love in Action . . .

Identify one area of your life where you've been putting off growth until you're married (finances, health, spiritual habits). Take one small step today to invest in that area, trusting that this season has purpose.

This waiting season isn't wasted; it's a time of growth and preparation.

WEEK

5

LEARNING PATIENCE IN THE UNKNOWN

If we look forward to something we don't yet have, we must wait patiently and confidently.
ROMANS 8:25

Everything I thought my future would be was shattered in an instant when my engagement ended. Now, just over one year later, God had led me across the country to California, far from home, far from family, and more alone than I'd ever felt.

I can still picture myself unpacking boxes in that tiny studio apartment, eating a simple dinner of lentils and cucumbers, the hum of the refrigerator echoing in the silence. At first, all I noticed was the emptiness: the chair beside me, the blank walls, the ache of wondering if God had forgotten my story.

But slowly, He began teaching me to shift my focus. Instead of staring at what was blank and missing in my life, I turned toward Him. I started covering my walls with pictures, Bible verses, and reminders of God's promises. It wasn't just decorating; it was choosing to believe His Word over the lies of loneliness. Each verse taped to the wall became a seed of patience and hope.

I still wrestled with questions: *Did I miss something? Am I going to be alone forever?* But in those quiet nights alone, God was shaping something deep within me. Patience. I learned that patience isn't passive. It's trusting that even when I can't see the next chapter, He is still writing it.

Looking back now, I see that what felt like emptiness was actually holy ground. In the very place I felt forgotten, God was planting roots of faith and patience in me that would one day sustain me in marriage.

Dear heavenly Father, *thank You for being a God who sees me even when I feel forgotten. You know the places where waiting feels hard and lonely. I lift up my future husband to You right now. If he's weary in the waiting, would You renew his hope and remind him that You are still writing his story? Encourage him where he feels weak and surround him with Your presence. Help him wait on You and not give in to the enemy's lies.*

Do the same for me, Lord. Guard me from filling the ache of waiting with distractions and instead draw me closer to You. Build in me the kind of patience that grows strong faith, so that when You bring my future husband and me together, our marriage will be rooted in trusting You. In Jesus' name, amen.

Love in Action . . .

Next time you feel anxious about the unknowns of your love story, pause and take three deep breaths. Speak this truth out loud: "God is still writing my story, and I choose to rest in His timing."

Patience grows when I trust the Author of my story.

WEEK

6

DELAYED DOESN'T MEAN DENIED

The Lord isn't really being slow about his promise, as some people think. No, he is being patient for your sake. He does not want anyone to be destroyed, but wants everyone to repent.

2 PETER 3:9

One of my favorite memories my husband, Caleb, tells about our love story is the very first time he noticed me at church. I was in the middle of worship, hands lifted, completely focused on Jesus. Across the room, Caleb saw me. He says it was like time froze—his own movie moment where the world stopped spinning and all he could see was me.

After the service, I went across the street to the little coffee shop our church owned. Caleb walked in too, and I remember noticing a really tall, very handsome man who carried himself with humility and a little shyness. We started talking, but right then, the guy I had just started dating walked up and put his arm around me. Caleb later joked about the stink face that guy gave him.

Caleb walked away that day knowing I was the girl he had prayed for. And he kept praying every day for me—for God's best, whether that was with the guy I was dating or with him. Meanwhile, I stayed in that relationship for months, trying to make it work. But the truth is, I kept having the nagging feeling he wasn't God's best match for me. The Holy Spirit kept convicting me, and with the help of a friend, I was able to break off that relationship. Caleb kept waiting and praying and telling his friends about his "dream girl." That still makes my heart flutter, thinking about what was happening behind the scenes that I had no idea about.

When I finally let go, God opened the door for Caleb and me to reconnect. And this time, the timing was right. Looking back, I can see so clearly the delay wasn't denial. It was God's way of protecting us and preparing our hearts for something so much better.

Heavenly Father, *thank You that You are never slow, even when it may feel that way. Your timing is perfect. I pray for my future husband. If he feels impatient, remind him that Your plan is still unfolding for him too. Encourage his heart and protect him from settling for less than Your best. Help him to look at other delays in his life where he has seen Your hand moving.*

Encourage me in the same way, Lord. Teach me to trust that delays are never wasted. They make us stronger, closer to You, and ready for each other. Help us to see how faithful You are. When You bring us together, let our love be built on the foundation of Your love. In Jesus' name, amen.

Love in Action . . .

Write down one prayer that has felt delayed in your love life. Beside it, write a reminder of a time God answered a prayer in your past. Let His past faithfulness give you hope for the future.

A delay from God is never denial.
It's redirection toward His best.

WEEK

GOD'S TIMING BRINGS FREEDOM 7

God has made everything beautiful for its own time. He has planted eternity in the human heart, but even so, people cannot see the whole scope of God's work from beginning to end.

ECCLESIASTES 3:11

After I broke things off with the man I had been dating, God began healing me in deep ways. I didn't feel like a shell of a person anymore. I was lighter, freer, and more myself again. That's right when Caleb reappeared in my story.

I saw him at church one Sunday, and something in me felt instantly at ease. I invited him to our church's Fourth of July picnic. Caleb told me later that he would have canceled any plans just to be there if it meant spending time with me.

The day of the picnic was simple but significant. We sat side by side in the grass, laughing and talking while fireworks popped in the distance. Our conversation wasn't forced. I didn't feel like I had to prove myself or perform. With Caleb, I could just be me. And Caleb told me later that he had felt the same—safe, seen, and full of joy.

Looking back, we both see how God's timing had been so intentional. If we had connected sooner, we might not have been ready. But when God brought us together at exactly the right time, it was beautiful. His timing always is.

Dear one, it's easy to be like a mouse in a maze when it comes to dating and relationships. All you see is the wall in front of you. But God sees the whole picture. You can trust Him to lead you the right way, get you unstuck, and ultimately reveal what you have been looking for.

Dear heavenly Father, *thank You for making all things beautiful in Your timing. You are the God who sees from beginning to end. Thank You for preparing my heart and my future husband's heart for the day You'll bring us together. I pray for him right now. Let him walk in freedom, confidence, and joy so he feels safe to be fully himself.*

Please do all the same things for me, Lord. Heal me of anything that makes me hide or strive, and help me live at ease in who You've called me to be. When the timing is right, let our marriage be filled with the peace and joy that comes only from You. In Jesus' name, amen.

Love in Action . . .

Think of one area where you feel the need to "perform" to be loved. Ask God to help you release it, and practice resting in His love today.

God's timing makes love feel like freedom for both of us.

Father, thank You
for Your perfect timing.
Encourage my future husband's
heart and mine, and teach us
to trust that delays are
never wasted.

WEEK

8

PREPARING TO HONOR YOUR FUTURE HUSBAND

Again I say, each man must love his wife as he loves himself, and the wife must respect her husband.

EPHESIANS 5:33

For a long time during my single years, I didn't really think about how my actions made guys feel. Flirting brought me attention, and attention made me feel valuable, but I wasn't considering whether my words confused them, built them up, or tore them down.

After my sophomore year of college, God began reshaping how I viewed men. He showed me they weren't just "tough" or "surface level." They were created in His image, with real feelings and worth. From that point on, I started practicing something new in my interactions with men: honor.

When I lived alone during seminary in Pasadena, California, I set boundaries, including not letting a guy into my apartment if we were alone and always being clear about my intentions. But it wasn't just about the boundaries. It was about learning to see men through God's eyes and honoring their character. I practiced speaking life into classmates and professors in a professional, respectful way. I chose to affirm the good I saw instead of letting sarcasm or indifference have the last word. Little by little, God was preparing my heart for marriage.

Because here's the truth: Marriage isn't just about love; it's about teamwork. It's about respecting and encouraging the strengths God has put in your husband while also bringing your own. When we honor men rightly as brothers, mentors, pastors, or friends, we are not only lifting them up but practicing the very skills that will make us trustworthy, supportive partners later on.

Heavenly Father, *I praise You as the God who created men and women to complement one another in love and partnership. Thank You for showing me that honor is preparation and that the way I treat men now sets the stage for how I will one day partner with my husband.*

I pray for my future husband. Teach him to lead with humility, to love with patience, and to carry strength with tenderness. Guard him from discouragement and surround him with people who call him to a higher standard. Prepare his heart not only for love but for respect, and to receive that respect with gratitude and grace.

Lord, shape my heart to practice honor now in every relationship—with friends, mentors, and brothers in Christ. And let me be a wife in the future who makes her husband feel respected and cherished. Please help our future marriage be marked by true partnership, where love and respect flow together, and teamwork that reflects the beauty of Christ and His church. In Jesus' name, amen.

Love in Action . . .

Think of one godly man in your life (pastor, brother, mentor). Send him a quick note of encouragement, practicing what it means to honor others.

When I learn to honor men now, I prepare to honor my husband later.

WEEK

9 CONVICTION AND CONFESSION

If we confess our sins, he is faithful and just and will forgive us our sins and purify us from all unrighteousness.

1 JOHN 1:9, NIV

Soon after Jesus captured my heart in college, shameful memories I had buried came rushing back: times I had crossed lines with boyfriends, moments when I had given away pieces of myself that were meant for marriage. For years, I brushed those regrets under the rug, but when the Holy Spirit showed me His holiness, the weight of my sin crushed me. I felt filthy and unworthy of God's love.

Maybe you've been haunted by memories you wish you could erase. The enemy loves to chain us to shame, whispering that we're too far gone. But by God's grace, Jesus doesn't leave us there. One night in college, I fell to the floor in shame, tears spilling fast. With shaking hands, I covered my face and whispered confessions, one by one, every sin that I thought disqualified me. But something incredible happened. With each confession, I felt the weight of my shame lift. It was like I laid down a heap of ashes, and Jesus handed me beauty. Scripture says He removes our sins as far as the east is from the west, and in that moment, I believed it (see Psalm 103:12). For the first time, I felt clean. I felt free.

Confession didn't just release me from shame; it opened the door to intimacy with God. And it still does today. Every time we confess our sins, He forgives us fully and loves us completely.

Sister, your sin and shame are not too much for Jesus. He came for this very reason, to carry every secret, every failure, every wound. And still today I practice confession when I fall short, because He is faithful to forgive and cleanse me again and again. Nothing else can purify our hearts like His love.

Father, *thank You for being faithful to forgive. Thank You that the blood of Jesus has covered my every sin and washed me clean. Thank You for turning shame into freedom and ashes into beauty.*

I pray for my future husband. Guard his heart and mind, Lord. Free him from the lies of the enemy and from any shame from his past. Give him courage to confess quickly and walk in the freedom You offer. Heal any places in him that still ache, restore his confidence in You, and shape him into a husband who leads with honesty, humility, and grace.

Lord, help me to live freely in You. Don't let shame or regret hold me back from the joy You've called me to. Teach me to walk as a woman forgiven, whole, and confident, so I can one day be a wife who loves with tenderness and strength. And Lord, give me and my future husband courage to invite You into the parts of our stories that still ache. Heal our memories and wounds. Redeem them with Your love and bind us together as two people who know the beauty of forgiveness and the freedom of living fully loved by You. In Jesus' mighty name, amen.

Love in Action . . .

Set aside five minutes today to confess one area where you've fallen short. Write it down, pray over it, and then rip it up as a reminder that God has fully forgiven you.

Confession clears the way for deeper intimacy with God.

WEEK

GROWING IN INTEGRITY 10

If you are faithful in little things, you will be faithful in large ones. But if you are dishonest in little things, you won't be honest with greater responsibilities.

LUKE 16:10

I sat in the middle of the floor with clothes scattered all around me. I had pulled everything out of my closet and drawers before my move to California. As I looked around at the various items, I didn't just see clothes; I saw stories. I had worn this short skirt so that a guy would like me. I had bought these black pants so another guy would notice me.

Each piece felt like a mask I had put on to prove I was enough. I had spent so much time trying to gain the approval of others that I had lost sight of who God made me to be. And that's when God convicted me. It wasn't just about the clothes; it was about my heart.

That season became a turning point. God began teaching me that faithfulness isn't just about what's on the outside; it's about the small, hidden choices too. Choosing honesty in conversations. Choosing authenticity instead of exaggeration. Choosing to root my worth in Him instead of others.

As I walked out my faith, God was shaping me for Caleb. By the time we found each other, our masks were gone. He fell in love with the real me, the woman God was forming, not a version where I performed. Looking back, I can see how God was faithfully preparing me in the little things so I could be entrusted with more.

Friend, don't dismiss the small steps of honesty you're taking. God sees each one. Whether in friendships, at work, or one day in marriage, those little acts of integrity will become the foundation for the bigger things He has planned for you.

Lord, *thank You that You see me fully and love me completely. Thank You for teaching me that integrity in the little things matters to You. I pray for my future husband, that You would form in him the same faithfulness and authenticity so our marriage will be rooted in trust. In both tiny ways and big ways, grow him to be a man that desires to honor You.*

Help us to both be who You made us to be. Put people in our lives who don't normalize sin but call us to a higher standard. Teach us to walk in truth and integrity so that together we can be entrusted with greater things for Your glory. In Jesus' mighty name, amen.

Love in Action . . .

Identify one small area where you're tempted to perform or exaggerate. This week, practice choosing honesty instead, trusting that faithfulness in the little things shapes your character for the greater things God entrusts to you.

Integrity in the small things prepares me for God's greater things.

WEEK

11

SURROUNDING YOURSELF WITH GODLY COMMUNITY

Walk with the wise and become wise;
associate with fools and get in trouble.

PROVERBS 13:20

One of the most practical ways to position yourself for God's best is to plant yourself in a church community. Going to church consistently, serving on a team, and getting involved in Bible studies or small groups opens the door to meeting new people who are running after Jesus just like you.

When I first moved to California, I didn't know many people at all. I could have filled my weekends with going to bars, but instead, I chose to fill them with church. I went to multiple services during the weekend and attended worship nights and prayer gatherings because I wanted to surround myself with truth. I was hungry for God, and that choice shaped everything.

One of the churches I attended in California had an older congregation, and I loved the mentorship I received there. But I also knew I needed peers to walk beside me—people my age, in my stage of life, running hard after Jesus. So I sought out a church with a thriving young adult ministry. It was a place to gather and grow in community. There I found friendships, mentors, and ultimately Caleb, who I might never have met if I hadn't positioned myself to be in godly spaces.

Not every church will have a large young adult ministry, and that's okay. But it is worth being intentional, even if you have to drive farther to plant yourself where mentorship and friendships can thrive. Godly community sharpens your faith, surrounds you with truth, and positions you for the love story God has for you.

Dear God, *thank You for the gift of godly community. I pray for my future husband today. Please surround him with people who love You, speak truth to him, and call out the best in him. Place mentors in his life who will strengthen his faith, and give him friends who will encourage him to run after You wholeheartedly.*

Do the same for me, Lord. Help me stay planted where I can grow, be sharpened, and be held accountable in love. Lead me into relationships that help me become the woman You've called me to be.

And I pray over our future marriage. Build it on a foundation of community that honors You. Please give us mentors who guide us, friends who support us, and a church family that helps us stay rooted in Your truth. Let the people around us strengthen our relationship, and let our marriage reflect Your heart to everyone who walks alongside us. In Jesus' name, amen.

Love in Action . . .

Take inventory of where you're planted. Do you have mentors who challenge you and peers who walk beside you? If not, prayerfully seek out a church or ministry where you can be both encouraged and sharpened.

Planting myself in godly community positions me for God's best.

WEEK

12

BUILDING HABITS THAT HONOR GOD

As for me and my family,
we will serve the LORD.
JOSHUA 24:15

One of my favorite "dates with God" was the day I drove out to Whipple Dam while I was living in State College, Pennsylvania. I turned off my phone, carried only my Bible with me, and settled on the shore. Kids splashed in the water, their laughter carrying through the air. The sun kissed my skin, and I felt wrapped in God's warmth. More than anything, I felt His presence and closeness.

That day wasn't only about being still before God. It was about being attentive to His voice and listening to what He put on my heart. As I read His Word in my light-green Bible, I was highlighting and taking notes on all that He was sharing with me. On my way home, I noticed two cyclists stranded on the side of the road. Normally, I would have kept driving, but I felt the Holy Spirit nudging me to stop. I pulled over, helped them load their bikes into my car, and gave them a ride back to Penn State. It seemed like such a small gesture, but it felt holy, an ordinary Saturday turned extraordinary because I chose to listen and obey.

Moments like this taught me that walking with God isn't only about dramatic encounters. It's about the small rhythms of faithfulness: daily prayer, gratitude, Sabbath rest, and paying attention when He whispers. Those habits carried me through my single years and became the foundation for the kind of home and marriage I longed for.

Years later, Caleb and I went on a marriage retreat where we lost all phone reception. At first, it felt inconvenient, but soon it became one of the sweetest weekends of our marriage—unplugged, fully present with each other, and tuned in to God. We came home convicted: If we don't set rhythms for our home, the world will set them for us. That's why we now unplug from social media on the weekends and create space for God and each other.

Friend, the habits you choose now matter more than you think. A marriage isn't built on milestones like your wedding day. It's formed in the everyday choices: whispering prayers over dinner, forgiving quickly, choosing gratitude instead of complaint, and listening for God's leading in the little things. These rhythms may look ordinary, but with Christ at the center, they become holy ground. The home you dream of tomorrow is being shaped by the rhythms you choose today.

Heavenly Father, *I thank You that You are the One who builds our homes and shapes our lives. You are faithful in the small things, and You teach us how to walk in rhythms that honor You.*

I pray for my future husband today. Train his heart to seek You daily in Your Word, in prayer, and in gratitude. Teach him to value rest in Your presence more than the noise of this world.

Guard his time and attention so he can be fully present with You and with the people he loves. May his habits reflect faithfulness, integrity, and love for You in both the hidden and public moments.

Likewise, I would love Your help, Lord, to continue growing in holy habits, choosing prayer, Sabbath, and gratitude so that my life points to You. And I pray for our future marriage, that our home would be filled with Your Spirit, shaped by daily faithfulness, and a light to everyone who encounters us. In Jesus' name, amen.

Love in Action . . .

Pray over your home today, asking God to fill it with His presence. Then choose one small, intentional habit, like daily prayer, unplugging from your phone, or practicing gratitude, that you can begin this Week to better prepare for a marriage that honors Him.

The small rhythms I build today will shape the home I share with my husband someday.

WEEK

13

GUARDING YOUR HEART FROM TEMPTATION

Run from anything that stimulates youthful lusts.
Instead, pursue righteous living, faithfulness, love, and peace.
2 TIMOTHY 2:22

When I lived in my tiny grad school apartment, I had one sad little window, and it faced the garbage dump. As if that weren't bad enough, one of the tenants in my building loved fishing. And not just catching fish but bringing them home to eat. He'd clean the fish in his apartment and then dump the guts right outside my window. Within minutes, my whole apartment smelled like rotting fish stew. I tried candles, air purifiers, all the tricks I could find online. Nothing worked. The smell always crept back in.

It makes me laugh now, but at the time, it was awful. And honestly, it's the perfect picture of temptation. We can try to cover up our struggles with excuses and distractions, but if we let the source of sin sit right outside our hearts, the stink will always come back in. The only solution? Get rid of it.

Guarding your heart isn't about being too strict or missing out. It's about protecting the purity and peace God wants for you. Just like I couldn't live in my apartment without dealing with the smell, you can't live in freedom without removing the source of your temptation. Get rid of the rot and instead let God lead you on a path of "righteous living, faithfulness, love, and peace."

Lord, *thank You that we have the aroma of Christ when we are close to You! Guard my future husband's eyes, thoughts, and heart from temptation. Give him the strength to flee temptation and the courage to walk in holiness. Help him to grow in purity and to see people as Your beloved creation.*

And Jesus, please protect me in all the same ways. Help me choose purity in my own life, not out of fear but out of love and respect for You. Remind me to run to You when I feel weak and to fill my mind with what is true, honorable, pure, and lovely.

I pray for our future marriage. May it have the scent of Your love and grace. Build a covenant between us that is faithful, guarded, and strong: a marriage that honors You and shines as a witness of Your love. In Jesus' name, amen.

Love in Action . . .

Identify one area of your life where temptation tries to creep in (social media, TV shows, conversations, habits). Take one concrete step today to remove the "source of the smell," whether that means unfollowing accounts, canceling streaming networks, or setting a boundary. Replace that habit with something that fills your spirit with life.

Purity isn't about restriction; it's about freedom and peace in Christ.

Father, build a future
covenant between us
that will honor You
and shine as a witness
of Your love.

WEEK

14

A RAINBOW OVER OUR YES

I have set my rainbow in the clouds, and it will be the sign of the covenant between me and the earth.

GENESIS 9:13, NIV

Every good and perfect gift is from above.

JAMES 1:17, NIV

Caleb had been leaving me roses and handwritten notes all week, each one a clue leading to "a special adventure." I had butterflies the whole time. I just knew something big was coming. The morning finally arrived, and it was pouring rain across Los Angeles. But as we drove along the Pacific Coast Highway toward Malibu, something incredible happened. Every time we got out of the car, the rain stopped. Every time we got back in, it started again. It felt like God Himself was clearing the sky just for us.

The whole day was filled with special adventures. We hiked through Solstice Canyon, explored the Getty Villa, and had lunch overlooking the ocean at Santa Monica Pier. It was one of those days that felt kissed by God, peaceful, fun, and full of laughter.

That evening, we drove to Crystal Cove, the same beach where we had first said, "I love you." The beach was empty, the sand smooth from the rain. Caleb carried his tripod down to the water, pretending to set up for a picture, and then turned toward me. His voice got quiet as he started telling me how sure he was that God had brought us together. Then he got down on one knee and asked, "Will you marry me?"

I said yes through tears and laughter. When I threw my arms around him, I looked up, and there it was. A huge rainbow stretched across the entire sky, glowing over the ocean like God had painted it just for us. We both stood in awe, laughing and crying at the same time, completely overwhelmed by God's goodness.

God doesn't give everyone a rainbow for their engagement, but He does have a way of blessing each story in the way our hearts will recognize. That day, the rainbow was His way of whispering, "I see you." However He chooses to show it, know His love is always near. Keep looking for Him, and you'll see His fingerprints all over your life.

Heavenly Father, *thank You for being so intentional with how You write our stories. You are the Giver of every good and perfect gift, the One who turns ordinary moments into reminders of Your love. Thank You that You know exactly how to surprise us, comfort us, and bless us in ways that reflect Your heart.*

I lift up my future husband to You. Surround him with Your presence, strengthen his faith, deepen his gratitude, and remind him that You are preparing something beautiful for his life. When You bring us together, let our love be full of joy, laughter, and reverence for You. May our relationship always point back to Your faithfulness and bring glory to Your name.

Thank You for being a God who still paints promises across the sky. I choose to trust that You are writing something beautiful, one detail at a time. In Jesus' name, amen.

Love in Action . . .

Pause today to thank God for one specific detail in your life where you see His love written clearly. Speak your gratitude out loud and let it shift your heart toward wonder.

When God writes your story, His promises shine through every detail.

WEEK

15

PREPARING SPIRITUALLY AND FINANCIALLY FOR MARRIAGE

If you are untrustworthy about worldly wealth, who will trust you with the true riches of heaven?

LUKE 16:11

There is a scene in John 12 where Mary takes a jar of perfume worth a year's wages and pours it on Jesus' feet. Judas Iscariot, who is present with them, criticizes her for being wasteful. But Jesus sees Mary's act as an offering of love. That moment in Scripture reveals something powerful: How we steward our money reveals our heart.

That's why financial choices aren't just practical but deeply spiritual. What we spend our money on shows what we value most. One of my clients, Kristi, knows this firsthand. After her husband left her for a younger woman, she was tempted to believe the lie that her value was in her body. She thought plastic surgery might make her more desirable and considered the expense. But after seeing one of my reels, she decided to invest in healing her heart instead. She booked a call with me and joined a course I ran to help women heal from past relationships and walk into the best future God has for them. During that time, God met her in her pain and anchored her identity in who she is in Christ. Not long after, she met an amazing man who adores her and loves her deeply, and together they serve God today. He cherishes her not for her body but because of who she is in Christ. Their marriage is such a redemption story.

It's amazing to see how surrendering our finances to God can change the course of our lives. Money can either feed insecurity or fuel transformation. When we invite God into every financial decision, we not only honor Him, but we also prepare our hearts and future homes to be built on wisdom, trust, and generosity.

Dear one, it's not wrong to put money into beauty, but if the motive is your negative self-worth, you will always feel empty. Instead, consider the resources God has given you and seek His wisdom in financial choices. Let Him fill your heart with His blessings.

Heavenly Father, *thank You for providing everything I need. I pray for my future husband, that You would shape his financial decisions with wisdom and generosity, preparing him to lead a household that honors You. Help his heart heal from any misconceptions he might have about money. Will You help him to trust You as his provider? Let him lean on You in his weakness so he can provide for our future family. Set him up now to make good decisions to bless our future.*

Teach me to faithfully steward what You've entrusted to me, to say no to things that feed insecurity and yes to investments that glorify You. Help us to put more money into things that will last into eternity. May our future marriage reflect a life of trust, generosity, and devotion. In Jesus' mighty name, amen.

Love in Action . . .

Before making your next purchase, pause and pray, *Lord, give me wisdom to steward what You've given me.* Let Him redirect your treasure toward things that glorify Him and grow you.

Where I put my treasure, I shape my heart, so I choose to invest in what glorifies God.

WEEK

16

CALLED TOGETHER

Two are better than one, because they have a good return for their labor: If either of them falls down, one can help the other up.

ECCLESIASTES 4:9-10, NIV

When Caleb and I first got married, we dreamed of going to Europe. We were both teaching at a small Christian school, pinching pennies and saving for the trip of a lifetime. But deep down, another dream was growing in my heart: to start a ministry that would help people know Jesus more deeply, heal from their past, and build godly marriages.

I'd mentioned that dream often, but one night it came out differently. I told Caleb, "I really feel like God is calling us to start this ministry now." He didn't fully understand the vision yet, but he believed in me. Instead of using our savings for the trip, we invested the money into something eternal—business classes, a camera, and other tools we needed to share the gospel online.

We both quit our teaching jobs at the same time, two steady paychecks gone overnight, because we knew God was calling us to take this leap of faith. As we built the ministry together, we both came alive. We grew closer through filming, editing, writing, praying, and learning together.

That little Europe fund we once gave up became seed money for something so much greater. And twelve years later,

God brought the dream full circle. He took us to Europe! While we were there, a woman named Cassie recognized us and let us know that our videos had changed her marriage. We stood by the River Thames, talking with her and praying together. It was one of those holy moments where you just know God is saying, "See, the seeds you planted are never wasted." The trip we once gave up became the very place where God showed us the fruit of our obedience.

Father, *thank You for calling us to dream with You. Thank You that when You bring two people together, You don't just give them love, You give them purpose.*

I pray for my future husband. Teach him to listen for Your voice and to dream courageously. Stir his heart with vision for the kind of legacy You want us to build together. Give us unity, clarity, and faith to move forward even when the path feels uncertain.

Lord, let our future marriage reflect Your Kingdom, as a partnership that serves faithfully and keeps You at the center. Thank You for the gift of dreaming together with You and for You. In Jesus' name, amen.

Love in Action . . .

Write down a dream you'd love to share with your future spouse. Pray over it this week, asking God to align your hearts with His purpose.

When two hearts chase God together, He turns shared dreams into lasting purpose.

WEEK

17

SURRENDERING FAMILY WOUNDS TO GOD

You turned my wailing into dancing; you removed my sackcloth and clothed me with joy.

PSALM 30:11, NIV

Anyone who belongs to Christ has become a new person. The old life is gone; a new life has begun!

2 CORINTHIANS 5:17

Some of the deepest wounds we carry come from the people we love most: our own family. For me, one of those wounds came when I was a child and was struggling to receive my dad's love.

My dad worked as a bricklayer, spending long days in grueling hard labor. I can still picture him coming home with mud on his clothes and exhaustion in his eyes, his hands rough and calloused from his work. Because he was a quiet man and didn't express love through words, I often misunderstood him as being hardened or stiff. What I couldn't see was that even after long days of work, he poured out his love for me through acts of service: filling my gas tank, fixing what was broken, paying for things I needed, and putting money away to invest in my future. He sacrificed much so that I could have more. But because my love languages were words of affirmation and quality time, I didn't recognize his love. I misread the story and believed the lie that I wasn't really loved.

Years later, while earning my master's degree, I read *The 5 Love Languages* by Gary Chapman. Suddenly, everything clicked. My dad had been showing me love all along; I just didn't know how to receive it. I broke down weeping, sorrowful for the years I had misunderstood him yet overflowing with joy because God was opening my eyes and expanding my heart to see love in a whole new way. That moment became a doorway for God's healing.

Friend, maybe you have your own family wound. A parent who didn't know how to show love in the way you needed. A sibling who hurt you. Or silence that left you feeling invisible. Whatever your story, God is faithful to redeem it. He can turn even the deepest heartbreak into hope. He is the perfect Father who fills every gap, heals every wound, and makes us new.

Dear heavenly Father, *thank You for being the Father who heals the wounds I carry from my family. Thank You for showing me that even when love isn't expressed in the way I long for, You are still writing a bigger love story over my life.*

I pray for my future husband, that You would bring healing to any family wounds in his heart and show him how deeply loved he is by You. Together, may we see the people in our lives through Your eyes. We ask that You enter into our hurt so we don't carry any negative patterns into our marriage. Teach us to bring our pain to You so it doesn't define our future but instead refines us to love each other with compassion and hope. May our marriage be a testimony of Your power, and may we speak each other's love languages out of care and compassion for the other. In Jesus' name, amen.

Love in Action . . .

Think of one painful family memory that still affects you. Write it down and invite Jesus into it, asking Him to show you where He can bring hope and healing into that place.

God heals family wounds and transforms them so we may have a deeper capacity to love.

WEEK

18

THE GIFT OF GRATITUDE

Always be joyful. Never stop praying.
Be thankful in all circumstances, for this is God's
will for you who belong to Christ Jesus.
1 THESSALONIANS 5:16-18

Caleb drove with one hand on the wheel and the other holding mine. I thought, *This is what love is supposed to feel like.* We were on a date driving down the Pacific Coast Highway. The date began with singing, talking, and enjoying the beauty of God's creation. For once I had a deep peace in my heart, not the anxious striving or uncertainty I once knew, but a calm, steady joy that only God could have provided.

Caleb switched the song on his iPod and said, "I want you to hear this one." "When I Say I Do" by Matthew West began to play. The lyrics began, "There must be a God, I believe it's true / 'Cause I can see His love, when I look at you." My eyes filled with tears. We had been dating for a number of months, but in that moment, I knew in my heart that this song was about me and Caleb. Gratitude swelled within me.

Not long after, another song came on, this one by Rascal Flatts, that felt like a song straight out of my journal. The lyrics sang, "God blessed the broken road that led me straight to you." The words echoed everything I was feeling. Each wrong turn and painful ending had been part of God's perfect rerouting. God led me straight into the arms of the man He had prepared for me.

We pulled over to the side of the road in Malibu to watch the sunset, our hands intertwined as the sky turned gold over the ocean. God's glory filled the sky, and we felt His faithfulness all around us.

Looking back, I'm reminded of Jesus' words in Luke 7:47, which express that those who have been forgiven much, love much. I feel this. All my mistakes, failures, and heartbreaks have made my love for God multiply.

A couple of months after this very special date, our dear friend Wendy sang "Bless the Broken Road" at our wedding, and tears filled the room. Every lyric was a testimony of God's faithfulness. Gratitude that began on that Malibu sunset drive became the foundation of our marriage.

Dear heavenly Father, *thank You for redeeming every part of my story and filling it with Your peace. Thank You for teaching me to look out for Your blessings every day and to be grateful for all the big and small moments. I lift up my future husband to You. Help him to walk in gratitude today and to see Your hand in every detail of his life. Let him count his blessings often and see our future marriage as such a gift.*

When we come together, may our love overflow with thankfulness, joy, and peace that reflect Your heart. Help us to see Your hand working in every part of our story. Let us never lose our sense of wonder for what You're doing in our lives. In Jesus' name, amen.

Love in Action . . .

Listen to a love song that reminds you of God's faithfulness. Let it become your prayer, thanking Him for how He's preparing your heart (and your future spouse's) through every season.

Gratitude opens your eyes to see God's love already at work in your story.

WEEK

19

GOD'S DREAMS ARE BIGGER THAN YOUR OWN

Just as the heavens are higher than the earth, so my ways are higher than your ways and my thoughts higher than your thoughts.

ISAIAH 55:9

When I was single and dreaming about my future marriage, I often pictured my husband and me as missionaries who traveled to villages, prayed for people under the open sky, and shared Jesus with those who had never heard His name. I longed for a marriage that would be about more than just us, one that would carry hope and freedom to others.

God did fulfill some of that dream. He's taken Caleb and me to El Salvador for a mission trip. But in other ways, He has completely rewritten the story. I never imagined that we would be "online missionaries," ministering to people across the world from our living room. Yet today, we've had the privilege of walking with clients in Uganda, New Zealand, India, Canada, Europe, Australia, and beyond. God took the desire of my heart to see people set free and reshaped it in a way I never expected.

One of the most powerful experiences I've had was working with a client who once taught pole dancing and kept a pole room in her house. As she and I worked together, the Holy Spirit convicted her to tear down the pole and transform the room into a place where women could meet for Bible study. The transformed space is now filled with Scripture and reminders of her identity in Christ. Here's the miracle: The women who now gather there don't know me personally, yet they are bearing fruit from seeds God asked me to plant and water. My client faithfully surrendered her heart to God, and now the women who meet there are growing in faith together. When I consider this, I realize that God's dreams ripple out far beyond what we can see.

Later, when I traveled to attend her wedding, I saw clients from around the world and people from our community who had once been strangers all together to celebrate. Different nations, different backgrounds, one family in Christ. It was a glimpse of heaven and a reminder that when we surrender our small dreams, God writes stories that bless generations. Friend, dream with God, and know that He wants to do immeasurably more than you could ever ask, think, or imagine.

Heavenly Father, *I thank You that You are the Dream-Giver and Dream-Fulfiller. Your ways are higher, Your plans are perfect, and You write stories that are better than anything I could ever plan for myself.*

I pray for my future husband. Fill his heart with God-sized dreams that go beyond his own comfort or ambition. Give him courage to surrender his expectations and follow wherever You lead. Enlarge his faith so he believes You in the impossible and let his obedience bring freedom and hope to others. Help me as well, Lord, to surrender my small dreams for Your greater ones, trusting that You see the whole picture even when I don't. I pray for our future marriage, that together we would walk in Your ways, living out a love story that impacts nations, generations, and every person You entrust to us. In Jesus' name, amen.

Love in Action . . .

Journal about one dream you have for your future marriage. Then ask God in prayer to reshape or expand it according to His greater vision.

God's dreams for me are higher, holier, and better than anything I could imagine.

Father, fill his heart with God-sized dreams that go beyond his own comfort or ambition.

WEEK

20

THE CALL TO GENTLE STRENGTH

When she speaks, her words are wise,
and she gives instructions with kindness.
PROVERBS 31:26

One of the things I value most in my friendships is honesty. Recently, I noticed a creeping lie trying to sneak into my mind about one of my best friends. We have always been supportive of each other's careers on social media by liking and commenting on each other's posts. But for a while, I noticed she hadn't engaged with mine.

It seems silly as I write it down, but it started to get to me. Lies began to swirl in my head. *Maybe she's upset with me. Maybe she doesn't value our friendship anymore. Maybe she doesn't think my content is valuable.*

After I prayed, God nudged me to be honest with my feelings. I realized how much I truly valued this friend and her encouragement. So I reached out and asked if I had done anything to hurt her and gently shared how I had been feeling. Her response was so sweet. She wasn't upset at all; she had just been busy. She actually thanked me for being honest and said she appreciated how much I valued her. That conversation brought us closer and gave us a new rhythm of encouraging each other in the future.

Friend, when emotions run high, I know how easy it is to react instead of respond or to shove things under the rug and quietly distance yourself. But gentleness is strength. Honest conversations, spoken with kindness, build the kind of trust that makes relationships thrive. Practicing gentle strength now is one of the best ways to prepare your heart for marriage later.

Heavenly Father, *I praise You for being a God who leads us with both strength and gentleness. Thank You for perfectly modeling honesty and love.*

I pray for my future husband. Teach him to be a man who uses his words wisely. Give him a gentle strength that listens before reacting and help him speak life even in moments of tension. Protect him from harshness or passivity and grow him into a man who brings peace to the people around him. Surround him with mentors who model courage and compassion.

Lord, help me to grow in all the same ways and to frame my words with gentleness, so I am building up instead of tearing down. Please let our future marriage reflect Your heart, as we learn to love with gentle strength that brings peace to our home. In Jesus' name, amen.

Love in Action . . .

Today, choose your words with intention and gentleness. Whether you're texting, at work, or with family, practice kindness. Doing so now prepares you to bring peace into your future marriage.

Gentleness is real strength that blesses marriage.

WEEK

21 DEVELOPING GODLY CONFIDENCE

God has not given us a spirit of fear and timidity,
but of power, love, and self-discipline.

2 TIMOTHY 1:7

At a Christian camp I attended, the speaker held up an image of the *Mona Lisa*. Then, right in front of the campers, he took a marker and defaced it, writing, "unloved," "not good enough," "failure," "worthless." He explained that the graffiti looked permanent but it hadn't destroyed the painting's true worth. In the hands of a master restorer, the damage could be removed, and the masterpiece would shine again. He started erasing the words and brought the painting back to its original beauty.

The speaker told us that we, like the *Mona Lisa*, are a masterpiece—God's masterpiece. The enemy and this world may try to cover us with lies, but those marks don't define us. Our value is untouched. And in the hands of our Master Restorer, every false label is washed clean.

That message healed a piece of my heart that day. Past words and actions had left their mark on me. But I was ready for Jesus to erase it all and make me into His masterpiece. When I returned home from camp, I surrounded my mirror with Post-it Notes of God's truth: chosen, beloved, beautiful, called. I filled my closet with Scripture. Everywhere I once looked and thought, *Not enough*, I replaced with His Word.

Slowly, my heart began to shift. The false labels began to fade, and His truth became what I chose to believe. That message has stayed with me through today.

Friend, you are God's masterpiece. Bring any past blemish or scar before Him and let Him fill you with His truth today.

Heavenly Father, *thank You that I am Your masterpiece and that no false label can diminish my worth. Thank You for giving me a spirit of power, love, and self-discipline, not fear or timidity.*

I pray for my future husband, that You would restore any places where he has carried hurtful labels. Help him to walk in faith and not fear. Let him know he is deeply loved and chosen Your son, bought at a high price—and allow him to see others in this same way.

Would You help me in these areas too, Lord? Help me to walk daily in godly confidence, and help our future marriage be rooted in Your Word, reflecting the security of Your love. In Jesus' name, amen.

Love in Action . . .

Write down three truths about who you are in Christ (chosen, beloved, called). Place them where you'll see them daily: on your mirror, in your journal, or as the background on your phone. When insecurity begins to whisper, speak these truths out loud and let God's Word cover every lie.

The world may graffiti your worth, but God always restores His masterpiece.

WEEK

22

CULTIVATING A SERVANT'S HEART

Even the Son of Man came not to be served but to serve others and to give his life as a ransom for many.

MARK 10:45

One of the sweetest things about my husband is how he constantly looks for ways to take a load off me and make my day easier. When I think of a servant-hearted man, I think of Caleb. Whether he's bringing me a glass of water, making me a snack, or packing up a bag for an adventure, his love is expressed in the small, thoughtful ways he serves me every day.

His acts of service remind me of a beautiful moment in Scripture. In John 13, Jesus gets up from the table where He was having supper with His disciples, wraps a towel around His waist, and begins washing His disciples' feet. The Son of God and King of kings takes the posture of a servant, bows down, and washes the dirt from His friends' feet. It shocks His disciples, but Jesus tells them He is setting an example: "I have given you an example to follow. Do as I have done to you" (verse 15).

That's what real love looks like—not demanding attention but giving it. Not asking what you can get but how you can give. When you choose to serve others now, you're training your heart for the kind of love that makes a marriage thrive.

Heavenly Father, *thank You for sending Jesus, who showed us that true greatness is found in serving. Thank You for the example of His humility and love. I pray for my future husband, that You would shape him into a man who loves to serve others with joy, following in the footsteps of Christ. Grow him today to serve faithfully and lead with humility.*

Teach me also to have a servant's heart, to love without keeping score, and to give without expecting anything in return. Please help our future marriage reflect the servant-hearted love of Jesus, so that we may bless not only each other but everyone around us. In Jesus' name, amen.

Love in Action . . .

Look for one way to serve someone today without expecting anything back. Serving others now will train your heart to love selflessly in marriage.

The best preparation for marriage is learning to serve with joy.

WEEK

23

DISCOVERING "MY WHY" FOR MARRIAGE

Where there is no vision, the people perish.

PROVERBS 29:18, KJV

One of the most transformative exercises I give my clients is to sit with God and ask Him, *Lord, what is Your dream for my future marriage? What do You want our relationship to do for Your Kingdom?* From that place of prayer, they write a simple "My Why" statement, a vision of what God has put on their heart for a godly future marriage.

The clients who do this faithfully are the ones who see their lives change. I've watched women who once felt stuck in a relationship or were tempted to settle suddenly become anchored in vision. They could look at a relationship and say, "This doesn't align with my why. I won't settle here." Some decided to walk away from men who weren't God's best match for them, and because they did, they later married amazing men who shared their vision for a marriage centered on God's Kingdom. Their why became their compass, keeping them aligned with God's dream instead of momentary feelings.

Having a vision doesn't mean holding on to unrealistic expectations; it means daring to dream with God. A Kingdom marriage isn't just about happiness; it's about impact and holiness. When you know your why, compromising loses its pull. You begin to see that saying no to anything less than God's best is really saying yes to His greater purpose for your life.

Heavenly Father, *thank You that You are a God of vision and purpose. Thank You that marriage is more than just companionship. It's a reflection of Christ and the church and a partnership for Your Kingdom.*

I pray for my future husband that You would give him clarity about his calling and prepare his heart to lead with vision. Help grow his vision for our marriage and the people You have called him to love and serve. Prepare our hearts now for a Kingdom-building marriage. May we live out our why, bringing glory to You, serving others, and leaving a legacy of faith. Help us not to forget, even in difficult seasons, that our marriage is for Your glory. In Jesus' mighty name, amen.

Love in Action . . .

Take ten minutes today to pray and write down your purpose for marriage. Ask God what He wants to do through your union to bless His Kingdom. Create a short "My Why" statement and keep it somewhere you can refer to it daily.

When I know my why, I gain the courage to say no to less and yes to God's best.

Father, shape him
into a man who loves
to serve others with joy,
following in the footsteps
of Christ. Grow him today
to serve faithfully and lead
with humility.

WEEK

24

NAVIGATING DATING APPS WITH DISCERNMENT

If you need wisdom, ask our generous God, and he will give it to you. He will not rebuke you for asking.

JAMES 1:5

One of my clients once showed me her dating profile. She's a kind, Christ-honoring woman, but the pictures she posted gave a completely different message. Unsurprisingly, the guys who messaged her weren't looking for commitment. They were only interested in a casual fling. She was left feeling frustrated and misunderstood because she wasn't attracting the type of men she hoped to date.

Another client had the opposite struggle. Her pictures were grainy and taken from a distance, making it hard to even tell what she looked like. She wasn't putting her best self forward. I encouraged her to invest in photos that felt feminine, confident, and authentic. When she did, her profile finally matched her inner beauty, and she began to show up for dates with joy.

Dating apps are geared toward attraction. When your profile reflects both purity and confidence, you give yourself a greater chance of meeting someone who values what truly matters. And when the wrong men don't pursue you? That's not rejection; it's protection.

Discernment in dating isn't just about the pictures you post. It's about prayer. Without it, dating can feel like chaos and confusion. With it, there's peace. Ask God for His eyes. Ask Him to help you see past polished photos and smooth words to what's real and lasting. His wisdom will guide you better than any algorithm. Seeing my clients set healthy time limits on dating apps, go in with prayer, and have accountability from friends is powerful!

Heavenly Father, *I praise You as the God who gives wisdom generously. Thank You for caring about even the small details of dating and for reminding me that You guide my steps.*

I pray for my future husband. Give him discernment to look beyond surface-level attraction and pursue what is good, pure, and lasting. Teach him to be authentic and intentional in every space he shows up, online or in person. Protect him from counterfeit connections and surround him with friends who call him higher.

Lord, shape my own heart to be wise and discerning so that I may reflect Christ in how I carry myself. Let me walk wisely and walk with You, inviting You into every moment and putting up boundaries to protect my intimacy with You. May my future marriage be built on wisdom and peace, a union guided by You from the very beginning. In Jesus' name, amen.

Love in Action . . .

Before you interact with men in person or online, pause and pray. Acknowledge God and who He is. Know how beloved you are. Ask Him to give you eyes to see others as He sees them and to help you be a blessing to those around you.

With God's wisdom, I can date with discernment and peace.

WEEK

25

OVERCOMING COMPARISON

Forget all that—it is nothing compared to what I am going to do. For I am about to do something new. See, I have already begun! Do you not see it? I will make a pathway through the wilderness. I will create rivers in the dry wasteland.

ISAIAH 43:18-19

There was a season when it felt like everything hit at once. The oven broke, our car needed repairs, and a tax bill came in that was far more than we had saved. It felt like one long week of bad news stacked on top of another. In that moment of exhaustion, the enemy whispered, "Wouldn't life be easier if you had chosen differently?"

I thought about friends whose lives seemed steady and secure—great jobs, new homes, plenty of margin. They didn't seem to worry about surprise bills or long nights of trusting God to provide. For a moment, I caught myself comparing our calling to theirs. But then the Lord reminded me of what truly matters. No amount of money or worldly stability could ever replace the gift of peace we've found in following His voice. Ministry hasn't always been easy, but it's been filled with purpose, laughter, and moments when we've seen God's hand in undeniable ways.

Comparison will always try to twist your view, making someone else's life look shinier or your path look smaller. But God's Word interrupts those lies: "Forget the former things. . . . See, I am doing a new thing!" (Isaiah 43:18-19, NIV). When we look back in longing or around at others, we miss what He's growing right now. The truth is every story has both beauty and struggle. And the life that looks effortless from a distance might have unseen battles behind it.

God is the Author of new beginnings. His grace covers the parts that feel unfinished, and His timing redeems what seems delayed. When I catch myself comparing, I remind my heart, *He's doing something new.*

Father, *thank You for reminding me that You are always doing something new. Thank You that I don't have to compare my journey to anyone else's because You are writing a story that is uniquely mine.*

I lift up my future husband to You. Guard his heart from comparison too. Teach him to find joy in Your provision and confidence in Your calling. Let gratitude mark both of our lives, even in seasons that feel uncertain.

Lord, forgive me for the moments I've looked to others instead of You. Heal the parts of my heart that still wonder, What if? *and help me rest in the truth that You're always working for my good. When the enemy whispers lies, remind me that You are my provider, my peace, and the One who makes rivers flow in dry places. In Jesus' name, amen.*

Love in Action . . .

When comparison creeps in, pause and whisper, "Lord, thank You that You're writing my story." Let gratitude bring you back to peace.

Comparison fades when your eyes are fixed on the God who's doing something new.

WEEK

26

DISCOVERING AND LIVING YOUR PURPOSE NOW

Whatever you do or say, do it as a representative of the Lord Jesus, giving thanks through him to God the Father.

COLOSSIANS 3:17

One of the excuses I often hear from clients is this: "I'll wait until I get married to start serving or pursuing my purpose." But why wait? Marriage isn't the starting line of your calling; Jesus is.

Think of Rebekah in the Old Testament. In Genesis 24, she wasn't sitting around waiting for marriage. She was out in the field, faithfully serving. When Abraham's servant approached her at the well and asked her for a drink of water, she went beyond his request and watered all of his camels too. It was in her service that she was seen, chosen, and brought into God's bigger story as Isaac's wife.

I've experienced this in my own life. Before I met Caleb, I wasn't holding back for marriage to begin living my calling. I was worshiping in church, mentoring youth, and pouring myself into the gifts God had given me. When Caleb first saw me at church, I was completely abandoned in worship to God. That was the moment he fell in love with me, a moment when my heart was fully alive in Jesus.

Sister, don't hold back your gifts until "someday." The very place you serve, the very dream you pursue, might be where

God not only grows your faith but also positions you to meet the one who will walk beside you.

Heavenly Father, *thank You that You have given me gifts, talents, and a calling right now. Forgive me for the times I've believed the lie that I should wait until marriage to step into my purpose.*

I pray for my future husband—that he, too, would live fully in his calling today, serving and representing You in all he does. Let him not believe the lie that his life begins after marriage. Help him to serve, use his talents for good, and grow to love You and others more every day.

Prepare us both to bring strength, passion, and vision into our marriage so that together we can glorify You in an even greater way. We want a Kingdom marriage that lives out the vision of serving and helping others You put in our path. Help us to share the gospel with others we encounter and be bold for You. In Jesus' mighty name, amen.

Love in Action . . .

Take one step today to live out your God-given gifts. Write a note of encouragement, serve in your church, or create something that reflects Him. Living purposefully now prepares you to bring your strengths and gifts into marriage.

Living with purpose today prepares me for a marriage of vision tomorrow.

WEEK

27

GOD HEALS THE WOUNDS NO ONE SEES

He said to her, "Daughter, your faith has made you well. Go in peace. Your suffering is over."

MARK 5:34

When I was younger, I experienced a wound that shaped me in ways I didn't understand at the time. A classmate hurt me deeply, and instead of knowing how to process it, I buried the pain and hardened my heart. I carried shame I didn't deserve and learned to protect myself by trying to stay in control. I used boys for attention and affirmation because it quieted the ache for a moment, but underneath my tough exterior was a girl who didn't know what to do with her pain. I felt unseen and unsafe, and I didn't know yet that Jesus cares about the wounds that no one else can see.

In Mark 5, we learn about a woman with a similar kind of pain. For twelve years, she's bled, living with a private wound that's drained her physically, emotionally, financially, and spiritually. She's tried everything the world has offered, yet nothing has healed her. Instead, her suffering has grown heavier with time. She knows Jesus is her final option for healing, and when she sees Him in a crowd and touches Him, she experiences a miracle. She stops bleeding. What moves me most is how Jesus responds to her. He doesn't just heal her body; He restores her identity. In front of everyone, He calls her "Daughter." Before anyone can label her unclean, unworthy, or broken, Jesus claims her as His. She isn't defined by her past, her pain, or her shame; she is defined by His love.

That same truth comforts me every time I think about the wounds I carried into adulthood. Jesus didn't turn away from me or wait for me to fix myself. He met me in my brokenness, spoke truth over the places I tried to hide, and slowly healed what shame had damaged. The same God who restored the bleeding woman's dignity and identity meets you in your hidden wounds as well. He sees what others have missed or overlooked. He knows the parts of your story you wish weren't there. And just like He spoke "Daughter" over her, He speaks beloved names over you.

This healing matters for your future, because healed hearts love differently. Healed hearts forgive differently. Healed hearts build strong, holy marriages that aren't shaped by fear or pain, but by wholeness. And the same God who is healing your heart is also able to heal the wounds your future husband carries so that your marriage can be built on truth, not trauma. Jesus is the only One who can take what feels like lifelong pain and turn it into a testimony of His compassion and power.

Heavenly Father, *thank You for seeing every hidden wound in my heart and loving me through each one. Speak "Daughter" over the places in me that still feel vulnerable or broken, and bring Your healing where shame once lived.*

I pray the same over my future husband. Lord, meet him in his wounds, restore what has been hurt, and remind him daily that he is chosen and deeply loved by You. If there are deep areas of pain he carries today, please meet him there. Give him the courage to reach out to You for deep healing work in all the places of his pain.

Prepare both of our hearts for a marriage built on wholeness, truth, and Your redemption. Let our story reflect the healing power of Your love. In Jesus' name, amen.

Love in Action . . .

Write down one hidden wound you've silently carried. Bring it to God in prayer, asking Him to speak His truth over that place. Replace the wound with the identity He gives you: chosen, beloved, restored.

God heals the wounds time can never fix.

WEEK

28

ROOTED IN CHRIST

Even before he made the world, God loved us and chose us in Christ to be holy and without fault in his eyes. God decided in advance to adopt us into his own family by bringing us to himself through Jesus Christ.

EPHESIANS 1:4-5

So much of my identity in high school was wrapped up in being "the girlfriend." I dated the quarterback and can still picture myself sitting at his table in the lunchroom, surrounded by his friends. People walking by saw it as the popular table, but inside, I felt lonely and invisible. One of his friends didn't even know my name, which confirmed what I was already feeling: My worth was tied to my boyfriend.

That belief led me to tolerate his mistreatment—lying, manipulating, and cheating. He walked in front of me everywhere we went as if I were an accessory to his life instead of someone to be cherished. I swallowed it all because I thought being chosen by him meant I was valuable. But looking back, there were nights I cried myself to sleep, mornings I woke up with a pit in my stomach, and many moments where I felt icky and small in my own skin.

Living for other people's approval always leaves us empty. That's why years later, a broken engagement ended up being one of the best things that ever happened to me. My world was shaken, but it forced me to see that my foundation wasn't supposed to be built on another person's attention. I realized I was standing on the Rock, a foundation that could never be shaken.

In my brokenness, Jesus met me with the truth I needed most: I wasn't forgotten or overlooked. I was already loved, chosen, and adopted into His family. My worth wasn't something I had to earn; it was already settled in Christ. And that truth changes everything.

Dear heavenly Father, *I praise You for being the God who loved and chose me before the foundation of the world. Thank You for calling me Your own and giving me an identity that can never be shaken.*

I pray for my future husband. Remind him that his worth is not in his achievements, his titles, or people's approval, but in being Your beloved son. Guard him from chasing affirmation in places that cannot satisfy. Speak Your truth into the deepest parts of his heart so he walks with confidence as a man chosen and adopted by You.

And Lord, I pray You will anchor me in the same truths. May I always know that I'm chosen and a daughter of the King of kings and Lord of lords. Even when feelings of rejection arise, help me know I'm never rejected by You.

May our future marriage be built on the unshakable foundation of knowing who we are in Christ. In Jesus' name, amen.

Love in Action . . .

Write out a short "I am" list from Ephesians 1:4-5 (I am loved, I am chosen, I am adopted). Read it over yourself each morning and night this week.

My worth is in the King of kings. I am chosen by God.

WEEK

29

MARRIAGE AS A REFLECTION OF CHRIST AND THE CHURCH

For husbands, this means love your wives, just as Christ loved the church. He gave up his life for her to make her holy and clean, washed by the cleansing of God's word.

EPHESIANS 5:25-26

Caleb and I stood on a balcony overlooking the sweeping coast of Melbourne, Australia. The endless blue of the Tasman Sea stretched out beautifully before us. We were there to officiate the wedding of one of our dear clients, someone I had walked with through both the heartbreaks and breakthroughs of her waiting season.

From the very beginning, Laura showed she was different. She woke up at three in the morning to attend our coaching calls. She flew across the world to attend our Wholehearted Love retreat, eager to become the woman God had called her to be. Even while she was waiting for her own prayers for marriage to be answered, she poured courage and hope into others, speaking life into them with such grace.

There were times when the thought *Maybe I'll never find a good guy* tried to take root in her heart. But instead of giving in to that fear, she kept walking with God faithfully. She chose to trust His goodness and timing. And in His perfect way, God brought her husband into her life.

On their wedding day, as Laura walked down the aisle toward Matt, it was clear this day wasn't just about two people falling in love. It was about God's faithfulness on display. Marriage is one of God's clearest reflections of Christ's love for the church. It's not shallow or selfish but sacrificial, forgiving, and enduring. It's a covenant that points a watching world to the gospel. Watching Laura and Matt begin their life as husband and wife, we were reminded again that marriage points beyond itself. It points to Jesus. And witnessing that in their story was one of the sweetest honors of our lives.

Heavenly Father, *I praise You as the Author of marriage and the One whose love is the perfect model of sacrifice and grace. Thank You for giving us the picture of Christ and the church to show us what a covenant marriage looks like.*

I pray for my future husband. Teach him how to love with the same selfless, steadfast love that Christ has for His people. Shape his heart to be gentle and strong, patient and bold, willing to lay down pride for the sake of love. Guard him from settling for the world's shallow vision of marriage and anchor him in Your design—one of covenant, commitment, and holiness. Surround him with godly men who will remind him of the sacredness of this calling.

Lord, prepare me to love with that same humility and grace, choosing daily to reflect You. Help me to trust my future husband as a leader and honor him with my words and actions. I want Your view of marriage, Father, so I ask that You keep shaping my heart. In Jesus' name, amen.

Love in Action . . .

Take a moment to pray Ephesians 5:22-28 over a couple you know. Ask God to strengthen their marriage and reflect His love through it.

A marriage rooted in Jesus reflects His love to the world.

Father, prepare both of our hearts for a marriage built on wholeness, truth, and Your redemption.

WEEK

30

THE POWER OF COVENANT VERSUS CONVENIENCE

Since they are no longer two but one, let no one split apart what God has joined together.

MATTHEW 19:6

Tell me I'm not the only one who orders stuff on Amazon just to see if it works. And if it doesn't? No problem. I just tape it back up and drop it off at Whole Foods, and the money is instantly returned to my Amazon account.

It's almost too easy. Our world makes returns simple, casual, and with no strings attached. But marriage was never designed to work that way. It was never designed to be a contract that could be returned or exchanged. Marriage is a covenant.

When Caleb and I officiated Laura and Matt's wedding, they requested we explain what biblical marriage means. We were more than happy to share. We stood before the wedding guests and said, "The world often treats marriage as conditional, temporary, and based on how we feel. But God designed it to be rooted in sacrifice, perseverance, and unshakable love."

That's why Paul says in Ephesians 5:25 that husbands are to love their wives the way Christ loved the church, laying His life down for her. That's covenant love. It forgives, endures, and keeps pointing the other back to Jesus. Wives reflect the church's devotion to Christ by honoring, trusting, and walking in unity with their husbands. As the two join together, marriage becomes a living testimony of God's faithfulness.

Laura and Matt's marriage ceremony became a silent sermon, a picture of Christ's love for the church. Your future marriage will carry that same sacred calling. It won't be built on convenience but rather will stand firm as a covenant. And with every prayer prayed together, every act of forgiveness, and every step of perseverance, you'll be showing the world what Jesus' love looks like.

Heavenly Father, *I praise You as the God of covenant love, whose promises never fail. Thank You for showing us through Your Son, Jesus, that true love is faithful, sacrificial, and enduring.*

I pray for my future husband. Ground him in the truth that marriage is not about convenience but commitment. Strengthen his heart to forgive quickly, endure patiently, and choose faithfulness over feelings. Protect him from the temptation to quit when life gets difficult, and surround him with examples of godly men who live out covenant love.

Lord, prepare me to be a woman who loves with that same perseverance and grace. Help me to know deeply what covenant love means. May our future marriage be a testimony of Your unbreakable covenant to the world around us. In Jesus' name, amen.

Love in Action . . .

Highlight today's verse in your Bible. Let it remind you that marriage is a covenant, not a casual contract.

Covenant love is built on commitment, not convenience.

WEEK

31 LOVE THAT LAYS ITSELF DOWN

You must have the same attitude that Christ Jesus had.
PHILIPPIANS 2:5

A few years ago, Caleb and I were out for a peaceful walk in our neighborhood, when suddenly a big dog charged down a driveway at us, barking, and with teeth bared. In that moment, my heart dropped.

Before I could react, Caleb instantly stepped in front of me. He squared his shoulders, stood his ground, and commanded, "No!" His body shielded mine as the dog skidded to a stop. The owner rushed out, yelling, and the dog backed down. I exhaled a shaky breath and whispered, "You protected me." Caleb simply replied, "Always." Seeing how he looked out for my safety, not considering his own, made my heart flutter.

The next morning, I woke up replaying that moment with gratitude. It hit me that this is exactly what Jesus did for us. He stepped in front of danger. He put His body on the line, standing between us and death itself. Even now, He intercedes, He protects, and He covers us even when we don't see the threat.

If I felt that safe with Caleb shielding me from a charging dog, how much more secure am I knowing Jesus has already stood between me and eternal death? That is covenant love. It shields. It sacrifices. It says, "I'll go first. I'll take the hit. You are safe with me." This is the love we have with Jesus and the love that your marriage will one day reflect too.

Heavenly Father, *I praise You as my Good Shepherd, the One who lays down His life to protect His children. Thank You for standing between me and the dangers I can't see, for being my defender and my peace.*

I pray for my future husband. Grow him into a protector who reflects Your heart. Give him courage to stand strong in the face of fear, wisdom to know when to step in, and a love that is sacrificial. Shape him into a man who covers, shields, and intercedes with both strength and gentleness.

Lord, teach me to rest in Your protection and to honor my future husband as well. Help me to lay my life down for him and care for him well. May our future marriage be a reflection of Your love. In Jesus' name, amen.

Love in Action . . .

Do one small act of selfless love today. Encourage a friend, let someone go first, or give your time and serve. Practicing humility now prepares you to love sacrificially in marriage.

Real love lays itself down for the good of another.

WEEK

32

FORGIVING THOSE WHO HAVE HURT YOU

Peter came to him and asked, "Lord, how often should I forgive someone who sins against me? Seven times?" "No, not seven times," Jesus replied, "but seventy times seven!"

MATTHEW 18:21-22

I'll never forget the sound of tiny rocks hitting the glass of my bedroom window in the middle of a freezing Pittsburgh night. I pulled back the curtain, and there he was: my first love, standing in the dark, begging me to let him in. And I did.

Dear friend reading this, forgiveness and reconciliation are not the same. If I could go back and sit with little Stefanie, that high school girl who fell in love for the very first time, I would wrap my arms around her and tell her she was worth more than she could imagine. She had already given him everything. She had been used, betrayed, and cheated on. And now, instead of walking away for good, she opened the door and let him back in. At the time, I thought love meant giving second chances at any cost. But instead of bringing me freedom, it left me bitter, ashamed, and even more broken.

Now, when I think of that night, I don't see just my younger self at the window. I see Jesus sitting beside me. I see Him forgiving the boy who hurt me, but more importantly, I see Him holding my face, whispering, "You are Mine. You are not disposable. You are My masterpiece."

Friend, think of the parts of your story where someone has hurt you, the memories you wish you could erase. Would you let Jesus step into those moments? Picture Him sweetly putting His hands over your hands, looking into your eyes, showing you the price He paid to forgive you fully. Feel Him lifting your chin, reminding you that you are deeply loved, fully forgiven, and empowered to walk in His love.

Forgiveness doesn't erase the wrong, but it does erase the chains. It loosens the grip of bitterness, heals the sting of betrayal, and makes space for love to flow again.

Father, *thank You that You are a God who forgives freely. Thank You that through Jesus, my sins are washed clean and I can extend forgiveness to those who have wounded me. Thank You for taking ashes and turning them into beauty.*

I pray for my future husband. Protect him from bitterness and resentment. Teach him to forgive quickly and deeply, just as You forgive. Prepare him to build a marriage with me that is rooted in grace, tenderheartedness, and unconditional love. Help him set the right boundaries to protect himself for Your best.

Lord, You know the tears I have cried, the nights I have questioned my worth, and the memories that still ache. Heal every place in me that was fractured by betrayal. Remind me daily that my value doesn't come from any human being; it comes from You. Help me protect my heart with Your wisdom and not let any person in who would draw me away from You and the future You have planned for me.

I invite You into the memories that still sting. Walk into those nights of pain with me. Sit beside the younger version of me who didn't know her worth. Redeem those moments with Your love and help me to forgive as You have forgiven me. In Jesus' name, amen.

Love in Action . . .

Close your eyes and picture one person who hurt you in a past relationship. Invite Jesus into that memory and then say out loud, "I release them into Your hands, Lord. Heal my heart so I can love freely again."

Forgiveness doesn't erase the memory, but it breaks the chains on my heart.

WEEK

33

WALKING WITH GODLY FRIENDS WHO SHARPEN YOU

Let us think of ways to motivate one another to acts of love and good works. And let us not neglect our meeting together, as some people do, but encourage one another.

HEBREWS 10:24-25

"Let's pray about it." Few phrases mean more when they come from a friend who continually points you back to Jesus. True friends aren't just companions; they are sharpeners. They motivate us to love God more, live with courage, and walk in truth.

I think of my friend Chelsea, who hardly ever talks with me without pausing to pray. She reminds me that prayer is always the best first response. I think of my friend Mandy, bold for Jesus, unafraid to stop in a restaurant or on a street corner to pray for a stranger. Her example gives me courage to love people more openly. I think of my friend Christy, a prayer warrior, who will cry with me in grief and celebrate with me in joy. And I think of those in my Bible study—Brennan, Eileen, and Tabitha—who push Caleb and me to step out in faith and listen for God's voice. I'm also grateful for another study I have with Justine and Jordan, who pray bold prayers and dive deep into Scripture, helping us to live it out.

These friends are answers to prayer. They've walked with us through pain, including the grief of losing our twins, and have lifted us when we felt too weak to keep going. Their voices have helped us overcome depression and reminded us to run toward Jesus.

This is why Hebrews 12:1 rings true in my heart: "Since we are surrounded by such a great cloud of witnesses, let us throw off everything that hinders and the sin that so easily entangles. And let us run with perseverance the race marked out for us" (NIV). Godly friends become part of that "cloud" cheering us on, spurring us forward, and helping us keep our eyes fixed on Jesus.

Good friends may not always be easy to find, but don't give up. When you do find them, treat them like gold. Thank them often, choose them wisely, and search them out with intention, because the right friendships will shape your walk with God and your future marriage more than you know.

Father, *I thank You that You place us in families of faith and surround us with friends who sharpen us. I honor You as the God who designed us to grow stronger together.*

I pray for my future husband, that You would bless him with friends who pray with him, challenge him, and encourage him to keep running after You. May he walk with men who call out the best in him, strengthen his faith, and keep him steady when life feels heavy. Protect him from voices that pull him down, and surround him with friendships that lift him closer to You.

Please give me the grace to invest in friendships that breathe life and stir my heart toward Jesus. Let me be brave and bold and mindful to put time and energy into good friends. Finally, plant my future husband and me in a community of friends who will pray with us, speak truth over us, and run beside us as we chase after You together. In Jesus' mighty name, amen.

Love in Action . . .

Text one godly friend and thank her for the way she challenges or encourages you. Strengthening friendships like this prepares you to build a strong marriage community.

Godly friendships sharpen me for godly love.

WEEK

34

RESISTING PRESSURE FROM FAMILY AND FRIENDS

Obviously, I'm not trying to win the approval of people, but of God. If pleasing people were my goal, I would not be Christ's servant.

GALATIANS 1:10

"When are you going to have kids?" If I had a dollar for every time someone has asked me that since Caleb and I got married, I'd be a millionaire. What most people don't realize is that Caleb and I have walked through pain and loss in this area. After miscarrying our twins when I was three months pregnant, questions about children have felt like salt in a wound. People don't mean any harm, but their words press on a tender place they cannot see.

Maybe you've felt that sting too. At family gatherings, holidays, or church events, the questions come: "Why are you still single?" "Have you met anyone yet?" They don't mean to hurt you, but their questions can feel exhausting and discouraging.

Here's what I've learned: The only safe place to bring that pain is straight to Jesus. Be brutally honest with Him about how much it hurts. He isn't shocked or disappointed by your honesty. When you pour out your discouragement, anger, or even jealousy before Him, He meets you with compassion. The sting of unmet longing becomes lighter in His presence because He's the Great Healer. He can handle your tears, questions, and pain for what hasn't happened yet. And as you let Him minister to you, your story begins to be shaped not by people's timelines but by His faithful hands.

Father, *thank You for being the One who sees my heart and holds my future in Your hands. You are kind, faithful, and good, and I choose to trust Your timing over people's expectations.*

I pray for my future husband, that he would not crumble under the pressure of others' opinions or questions. Guard his heart from discouragement and fill him with confidence to live faithfully in the season You have him in. Let him walk in peace, knowing that You are preparing him for marriage at the perfect time. Remind him daily that Your approval is all that matters.

I pray the same for me, Lord. Instead of shutting down or hiding my heart from You, help me to keep being honest with You. And when You join us together in marriage, may we be a couple who rests in Your timing and lives free from the weight of people's expectations. In Jesus' mighty name, amen.

Love in Action . . .

The next time someone asks, "So, when are you getting married?" gently reply with faith, "I'm trusting God's timing for my story." Afterward, bring your real feelings about the question to Jesus in prayer.

I don't live by people's timelines. I live by God's.

WEEK

35

DEALING WITH GHOSTING AND DISAPPOINTMENT

The Lord is close to the brokenhearted;
he rescues those whose spirits are crushed.

PSALM 34:18

One of my clients used to spiral every time a guy ghosted her. She'd replay their last text over and over again, wondering what she had done wrong. The silence crushed her. And while ghosting may feel like rejection, it's often God's protection. It's His way of removing someone from your life who was never meant to carry your heart.

Here's the truth: Your future husband won't leave you in confusion. He won't disappear without a word or keep you guessing about his intentions. He will pursue you with clarity and consistency, because that's what commitment looks like. Until then, when someone fades out of your life, you can release him with peace and rest in the fact that God is near to the brokenhearted. He is faithful to lead you toward His best.

Friend, ghosting and disappointments hurt, but they don't define you. They are not a reflection of who you are. Rather, they are a reflection of who the other person wasn't. Don't project past experiences on your future. Instead, turn to God and His plan for you.

Heavenly Father, *I praise You for being close to the brokenhearted and never abandoning Your children. Thank You for using rejection and silence from others to guide and protect me.*

I pray for my future husband. Make him a man of clarity and courage. Guard his heart from passivity or fear that would cause him to pull away or leave someone guessing. Teach him to communicate with honesty and respect, reflecting Your faithfulness in the way he pursues me. Protect him from discouragement in his own waiting and remind him of Your nearness.

Lord, teach me to see rejection through Your eyes—not as loss but as redirection. Help our future marriage to be marked by trust, honesty, and the kind of love that never leaves the other questioning. In Jesus' name, amen.

Love in Action . . .

When someone pulls away, remind yourself, "I want God's best and will say no to the rest."

Rejection is God's protection. Clarity makes room for God's best.

Father, surround him
with examples of godly men
who live out covenant love.

WEEK

36

ESCAPING THE TRAP OF COMPARISON ON SOCIAL MEDIA

Since we are surrounded by such a huge crowd of witnesses to the life of faith, let us strip off every weight that slows us down, especially the sin that so easily trips us up. And let us run with endurance the race God has set before us.

HEBREWS 12:1

Social media can be a blessing and a burden. When I first stepped into ministry in 2016, sharing the gospel and teaching about God-honoring relationships online, I quickly learned how sneaky the enemy can be in this space. Social media has a way of distracting us by pulling us outside of our purpose and into comparison if we aren't careful.

I think of my husband working in our yard. When we moved to a wooded area in Pittsburgh, Caleb bought a chainsaw to trim the trees along our property. When he uses it during the day, with a sharp blade and in the right conditions, it's an incredibly useful tool. But if he tried to use it in the dark with a dull blade, or when he was overtired, it could become dangerous really fast.

Social media is the same. Used wisely, it can encourage us, connect us, and point us back to Jesus. But used carelessly late at night when our hearts are tired, when we're endlessly scrolling, or when our spirits feel dull, it can cut deep. That's when the lies of the enemy slip in: *You're not enough. You're behind. Your story doesn't measure up.*

God has set a unique race before you. Comparison only slows you down. But surrendering to God's plan helps you run with endurance. When we put down the phone and look up, we remember that real abundant life is happening right in front of us.

Heavenly Father, *thank You for being my anchor when the world feels noisy and distracting. You are steady, faithful, and true.*

I pray for my future husband. May he walk in confidence in the race You have marked out for him. Protect his eyes, mind, and heart from the pressure to measure his worth against others. Instead, let him find his identity in You alone. May he use social media with wisdom and purpose, as a tool that brings encouragement, not comparison.

Help me also, Lord, to guard my own heart and keep my eyes fixed on Jesus. I want to honor You in every space I'm in, whether online or in person. Teach me to be more present and to set limits on anything that steals from my purpose. Prepare our future marriage to be a place where we celebrate each other's callings instead of competing, where we run side by side with endurance in the life You've designed for us. In Jesus' mighty name, amen.

Love in Action . . .

Limit your social media use to fifteen minutes today. Then take the time you'd normally spend scrolling and replace it with something life-giving, like reading Scripture, taking a walk, or calling a friend.

Less scrolling, more living. God fills me where social media can't.

WEEK

37

CHERISH: WHERE LOVE GROWS STRONGER

By wisdom a house is built, and through understanding it is established; through knowledge its rooms are filled with rare and beautiful treasures.

PROVERBS 24:3-4, NIV

Everything great takes effort. Movies end the moment the couple finally gets together. They never go on to show the daily choosing, the tending, the cherishing. Yet that's where real love grows. Romance can last a lifetime, but only when you choose to care for it.

Think of a beautiful, brand-new home. Perfect floors. Fresh paint. Sparkling counters. If no one maintains it—no cleaning, repairing, or attention given to it—it won't stay beautiful for long.

Love is the same. Caleb and I chose early on to be intentional in our marriage. We Sabbath together. We put our phones away when we curl up on the couch. We invest in counseling. We say yes to marriage retreats every year. We go on date nights, build traditions, and keep learning about each other as we grow. Not because we're perfect, but because we protect what matters. And the grass really is greener where you choose to water it.

Cherishing isn't only for marriage. It's a heart posture you begin long before you meet your husband. In marriage, cherishing protects unity. In dating, cherishing protects clarity. When you're dating, cherishing doesn't mean overlooking red flags or pretending someone is farther along than they are. It means honoring what's good without forcing a future God hasn't confirmed. It means appreciating who someone truly is while staying grounded, prayerful, and honest.

Gratitude keeps your heart soft. Wisdom keeps your heart safe. Learning to cherish now prepares you to love well later. Proverbs 24 says a house is built with wisdom and filled with treasures through knowledge. Relationships grow the same way. The treasures of a future marriage—patience, gratitude, gentleness, forgiveness—don't appear on their own. They grow where you choose to nurture them now.

Dear heavenly Father, *thank You that You continue to teach me and my future husband the secrets of a life well lived. Help us make You our priority. Teach us to honor the Sabbath, not out of legalism but out of a deep need for rest and connection with You and each other. Help us create rhythms of intention in our future marriage, to cherish You and one another. Let no root of bitterness grow. Help us pull out the weeds quickly with the Holy Spirit's help. Show us how to water the thriving parts of our relationship, to appreciate each other, and to call forth the good often. Bless my future husband. Help him become a man who desires to cherish me, and help me become a woman who cherishes him in return. In Jesus' mighty name, amen.*

Love in Action . . .

Choose one intentional act of cherishing today: gratitude, encouragement, or prayer. Water what you want to grow.

Love flourishes when you tend to it.

WEEK

38 JESUS, BE THE GUEST OF HONOR

Let us rejoice and be glad and give him glory! For the wedding of the Lamb has come, and his bride has made herself ready.

REVELATION 19:7, NIV

When we planned our wedding, we didn't just want a pretty day. We wanted Jesus to be the guest of honor. Not the "Caleb and Stefanie show," but the Jesus show. We were planning from across the country and on a budget, and every time I started to get stressed about the details, I reminded myself that Jesus was the One I wanted to honor. He would help us work out the rest.

The day of our wedding, it was pouring rain, with thunder, lightning, and a gray sky that felt like it would never break. Our ceremony was outside, yet I felt this deep peace. We had invited God from the beginning, and I knew His peace would cover everything.

Right when it was time for our first look and the ceremony to start, the rain stopped. We worshiped, shared vows, and looked out at all the faces who had been part of our story. Over and over again, people told us, "It felt like heaven on earth." And in the sweetest way, God held back the rain until every single person made it safely into the reception barn.

Here's the truth: Inviting God to be the focus, no matter what situation you are in, will calm your heart, shift your perspective, and help you give Him glory.

The world makes weddings feel like a performance: Be perfect enough, pretty enough, impressive enough. But when your focus changes from "How can everyone see me?" to "How can everyone encounter Jesus?" the pressure eases. There's so much peace when He's the One at the center.

And you don't have to wait until your wedding day to live like that. Every day is a fresh start to say, "Jesus, I'm all in for You. You're the guest of honor here." When you invite Jesus into the little moments, it becomes second nature to invite Him into the big ones too.

Dear God, *I don't want my life or my future wedding to be a show. I want it to be about You. Be the guest of honor in my heart, my home, my dating, my engagement, and my future marriage. Teach me to invite You into every detail, not just the big moments.*

I lift up my future husband to You. Draw him close to Your presence in his everyday life. Help him invite the Holy Spirit to lead in every decision. Let his ears be open to Your voice and his heart be soft toward You.

Help us see others through Your eyes, love like You love, and build a marriage that feels like a little slice of heaven on earth because You're at the center. In Your name, Jesus, amen.

Love in Action . . .

Before you plan anything today—a date, a wedding detail, a text, even your schedule—pause and say, "Jesus, I invite You in. Be the guest of honor here. Help me see this through Your eyes." Then pay attention to the peace, clarity, or direction He gives you.

When Jesus is the guest of honor, even an ordinary day can feel like heaven on earth.

WEEK

39

THE GIFT OF WISE COUNSEL

Without wise leadership, a nation falls; there is safety in having many advisers.

PROVERBS 11:14

The company you keep will shape the course of your life. Scripture says, "Walk with the wise and become wise" (Proverbs 13:20). Wise, godly friends can see things we sometimes can't see for ourselves.

Many years ago, I dated a guy who everyone in church seemed to rave about. People called him "the most eligible Christian bachelor," and at first I believed their praise. He even asked me to do premarital classes with him. But I soon learned that behind closed doors, he wasn't keeping his word, and I didn't have peace in moving our relationship forward.

I can still remember the internal battle. Was this lack of peace a warning from God, or was it just fear of commitment speaking? The battle between those voices was exhausting. Fear whispered that I was just being dramatic, while the Holy Spirit was quietly nudging me to pay attention.

One night, my friend Christy pulled me aside. With compassion in her eyes, she said, "That full-of-life Stefanie I know doesn't seem to be here anymore. Your abundant vibrance and joy have dimmed. This relationship is not bringing out the fullness of who you are in Jesus." Her words pierced me. In that moment, I realized God was confirming through Christy what He had already been telling me. Christy's voice gave me the courage to walk away.

Not long after, Caleb asked me out—the man who had been praying and waiting for me for a year. If I had stayed stuck in my indecision, I wouldn't have been ready for the love story God had written for me. Wise counsel doesn't replace the voice of the Holy Spirit, our greatest Counselor, but it often confirms what He's already speaking. That's why surrounding yourself with friends who love you and point you back to God is one of the greatest gifts you can give yourself.

Father, *I thank You that You are the Wonderful Counselor, the One whose wisdom never fails. I praise You for surrounding me with godly voices who point me back to You.*

I pray for my future husband, that he would walk with wise, godly friends who sharpen his faith and call him higher. May he have mentors who speak truth into his life, leaders he can trust, and friends who encourage him when he's weary. Protect him from counterfeit voices that would lead him astray, and give him ears tuned to Your Spirit.

Lord, help me as well to discern Your voice clearly and receive wise counsel with humility. Let me be fully obedient to You, even when it's countercultural or difficult. Surround my future marriage with trusted friends who will strengthen our union, encourage our faith, and remind us of Your truth when we forget. In Jesus' mighty name, amen.

Love in Action . . .

Reach out to a trusted mentor, pastor, or friend this week and ask one question about relationships or faith. Listening to their wisdom now will help guide you in marriage later.

Wise voices today protect me from regret tomorrow.

WEEK

40

CHOOSING PURITY IN A CULTURE OF COMPROMISE

Don't you realize that your body is the temple of the Holy Spirit, who lives in you and was given to you by God? You do not belong to yourself, for God bought you with a high price. So you must honor God with your body.

1 CORINTHIANS 6:19-20

I spun the small silver ring on my finger, the one with a tiny cross cutout in the middle. It didn't look like much, but it was one of my most treasured possessions. After Jesus radically saved me my sophomore year of college, I knew if I really wanted to follow Him, I couldn't keep living the way I had been.

That meant leaving behind anything that might cause me to compromise my values. It wasn't easy. But when the Holy Spirit filled me with His love, He also gave me the strength to say no to anything less than God's best. That ring became my promise to God: I would honor Him with my body until marriage.

I was no longer afraid to tell any guy I dated that there would be no sex before marriage. I changed the shows I watched, the music I listened to, and even the conversations I engaged in. Not because I wanted to be legalistic, but because I wanted my heart and body to honor and stay aligned with the God who had set me free. Did I always walk this out perfectly? No. But by God's grace, Caleb and I got to exchange that purity promise for something so beautiful in marriage.

On the day he proposed, Caleb slipped that simple silver band off my finger and replaced it with the stunning diamond I still wear today. On our wedding night, I felt deeply pure and cherished—not because of my own strength but because God had been faithful to guard what I had entrusted to Him. To this day, I still set boundaries around what I watch, listen to, and dwell on. Purity is not just about virginity; it's about devotion. It's about living every day in a way that honors God with your body and heart. Friend, the boundaries you set matter. Every no to compromise is really a yes to God's best for your life and future marriage.

Heavenly Father, *thank You that You are pure and holy and that You invite me to walk closely with You. Thank You for giving me the Holy Spirit, who strengthens me when temptation comes.*

I pray for my future husband. Guard his heart and help him say no when temptation arises. Put others around him who fight for purity. Let his pursuit of purity be reflected in his actions, what he watches, and what he listens to. Remind him that he is Yours. Chosen, loved, and set apart.

Help me in all the same ways, Lord. Help me to walk in purity, and may our future marriage reflect Your holiness and devotion. May we see each other through Your eyes—pure and made new—and never hold our pasts against each other. Let our marriage be a testimony of Your goodness! In Jesus' mighty name, amen.

Love in Action . . .

Choose one boundary today that honors God with your body. Maybe it's avoiding a show that stirs up lust, unfollowing an account that feeds temptation, or saying no to a situation that blurs the lines. Protecting purity now is one of the greatest gifts you can give your future marriage.

Every no to compromise is a yes to God's best.

WEEK

41

HAVING MENTORS WHO MODEL MARRIAGE WELL

Teach the older women to live in a way that honors God. . . . These older women must train the younger women to love their husbands and their children.

TITUS 2:3-4

I'll never forget one particular session with a client across the world. Tears streamed down her face as she shared her pain, but before she told me her complete story, the Lord gave me a vision. I saw her sitting on the bathroom floor, weeping. Jesus was beside her, wiping her tears. When I shared this vision with her, she broke. Though her father had left her, she realized that she had never been abandoned. God was with her, even in her lowest moments.

Moments like this remind me of the holy weight of mentoring. It's about God meeting people in their pain and bringing healing to wounds from past rejection, shame, lies, or sin. I've watched Him use these sessions to rewrite stories and prepare hearts for healthy, godly relationships.

It's also why I believe in mentors for myself. When I was single, I invested time and money into godly counselors who helped me heal from past wounds, identify my blind spots, and walk forward in freedom. I wanted to let go of old patterns that hindered my relationships. Later, when Caleb and I were dating, we took premarital classes because we knew we needed wise voices to shape us before we said "I do." Today, we have been married for several years and still get poured into from older godly couples.

Whether you're single, dating, preparing for marriage, or married, know that mentors matter. They help you heal, grow, and gain a vision for the kind of covenant love God has for you. Their faithfulness will give you hope, and their wisdom will help you in your next step.

Father, *I thank You for being the Wonderful Counselor and that through Your Spirit, You place mentors in our lives who bring wisdom, healing, and guidance. I honor You as the One who leads us into freedom and prepares us for covenant love.*

I pray for my future husband—that You would surround him with godly mentors who will teach him faithfulness, humility, and how to love with Christlike strength. Give him spiritual fathers who will pray with him, encourage him, and call out the best in him. Keep his heart open and teachable.

Help me remain humble and hungry to grow, always willing to receive wisdom and invest in the guidance You provide through mentors. Surround us with couples who will model covenant love, speak truth into our lives, and walk with us through every season. In Jesus' mighty name, amen.

Love in Action . . .

Prayerfully seek out a godly mentor or counselor. Be willing to invest your time, humility, and resources into learning from their example and guidance.

Watching faithful marriages shapes the vision for my own.

Father, help him become
a man who desires to cherish me,
and help me become a woman
who cherishes him in return.

WEEK

42

TRUSTING GOD WITH THE TIMING OF YOUR STORY

God has made everything beautiful for its own time.

ECCLESIASTES 3:11

One of my favorite people in the Bible is Joseph. His story speaks to me so often, especially in seasons of waiting. God gave Joseph a dream that he would one day rule over his brothers. But instead of walking right into that promise, he was first betrayed, sold into slavery, wrongly accused, and even thrown into prison. From the outside, it looked like terrible timing. From the inside, Joseph had every reason to grow bitter.

But what amazes me is that Joseph stayed faithful. In betrayal, he still listened to God's voice. In prison, he still walked in purpose. He chose forgiveness instead of revenge when his brothers finally stood before him years later.

I think about that when I look at my own story. After my broken engagement, I waited five years before meeting and marrying Caleb. My husband and I have now been married for more than twelve years, and though we've prayed and longed for a child, we've said goodbye to two babies who are now in heaven and we await a child on earth. Waiting is painful. It can feel like everyone else is moving forward while you're stuck in a prison cell.

But Joseph's life reminds me that waiting doesn't have to be wasted. Joseph drew closer to God in his waiting. He let God heal his bitterness and grow forgiveness in him so that when God's promise finally arrived, he was ready to carry it with love.

The same God who was faithful to Joseph is faithful to you and me. His plans are never rushed, never delayed, and always right on time.

Father, *thank You that Your timing is perfect and Your ways are higher than mine. You never fail to keep Your promises. I pray over my future husband today. Help him to stay steadfast in his waiting season, walking in integrity like Joseph, even when life feels unfair. Strengthen him to resist bitterness, and teach him to lean on You when his dreams seem delayed. Shape his character so that he reflects Your peace and faithfulness in every circumstance.*

Help me to also trust You fully with my waiting, surrendering my timeline to Yours. Help me not to complain or miss the purpose of my waiting season. And Lord, when You bring my future husband and me together in marriage, may our relationship be a living testimony that Your timing is beautiful and worth the wait. In Jesus' mighty name, amen.

Love in Action . . .

Write down three areas of your life where you feel behind. Then pray over each one, releasing it into God's timing and thanking Him that His plan is perfect.

God's plans are never rushed, never delayed, and always right on time.

WEEK

43

LEARNING FROM THE SPARKS THAT FLY

We know that God causes everything to work together for the good of those who love God and are called according to his purpose for them.

ROMANS 8:28

One night in our California apartment, Caleb told me to wait upstairs because he was planning a surprise date on our porch. I could hear soft music playing and smell something delicious cooking. Then I heard a loud pop and peeked over the banister. Huge flames shot up from our patio furniture.

I sprinted down the stairs, grabbed the fire extinguisher, and helped Caleb put out the blaze. He had lit tiki torches to make the moment romantic, but a spark had fallen on a cushion and ignited the chair in flames. The spark he had been trying to light got a little too literal.

Once the fire was out and the cleanup was done, we both burst out laughing. The evening had not gone as planned, but it's one of my favorite memories to look back on now. The truth is, so many moments in marriage—and life—turn out differently than we expect. Sometimes we make mistakes, and sometimes those mistakes feel big. But when we can still see the blessings in those moments, our perspective shifts and we learn and grow.

God doesn't waste even our missteps. He uses them to deepen patience, humility, and gratitude. That's what Romans

8:28 means to me. Even the sparks and near-disasters can work together for good when love and faith are in the center.

Corrie ten Boom once compared life to a tapestry. The backside looks messy and tangled, but when you flip it over, you see a crown, a beautiful design only the weaver could create. In the same way, we can't always see what God is weaving through our imperfect moments. But when we trust Him, even the tangled threads can become part of something beautiful.

Father, *thank You for using every spark and every mess-up to teach us grace. Help me see that mistakes don't define me; they refine me.*

I pray for my future husband. When things don't go as planned, give him peace instead of frustration. Teach us both to laugh easily, forgive quickly, and see the beauty You're weaving even through the chaos. Let our love story reflect Your patience, humor, and hope.

When we face moments that go up in flames, literally or figuratively, help us remember that You're still in control. You turn every spark into light when we place it in Your hands. In Jesus' name, amen.

Love in Action . . .

When something doesn't go as planned this week, pause and thank God instead of getting frustrated. Ask Him what lesson or laughter He might be weaving through it.

Even when everything seems to go up in flames, God can weave beauty from the ashes.

WEEK

44

BECOMING THE ANSWER TO SOMEONE'S PRAYER

Who can find a virtuous and capable wife? She is more precious than rubies. Her husband can trust her, and she will greatly enrich his life.

PROVERBS 31:10-11

"Caleb had your missing tooth!" My mouth dropped open as my mother-in-law, Kay, said those words across the kitchen table. We were gathered for our weekly meal at their house, surrounded by framed baby pictures of Caleb and his siblings, Kay's beautiful paintings, and the smell of her home cooking. I had just explained that I was getting braces to correct my bite, which would leave me with a missing tooth.

Kay smiled and explained how years ago, Caleb had an extra adult tooth in the very same spot. It was oddly shaped, so the dentist pulled it. The same side. The same tooth. It felt like a God-wink in the middle of a casual dinner.

My mind went back to the many times Kay had told me she and John had prayed for me long before they knew my name. I think about how they might have been lifting me up as a teenager when I was too insecure to smile or when cruel comments online made me want to hide. Now, here I was, holding Caleb's hand under the table, staring into his eyes filled with love, realizing God had written a story only He could write.

Mark 10:7-8 says, "For this reason a man will leave his father and mother and be united to his wife, and the two will become one flesh" (NIV). In marriage, Caleb and I are one. But even before we found each other, God was weaving our lives together. My insecurities that once made me feel unworthy of love became the very places God showed His faithfulness. He didn't just answer my prayers; He shaped me to become the answer to Caleb's prayers too.

God often answers prayers through people. Caleb's parents prayed for me for decades, and here I was, sitting at their table, an answer to the request they had long carried before God. Caleb prayed for a wife, and God was shaping me through years of waiting, healing, and daily faithfulness. And I prayed for a husband, not realizing God was already refining Caleb to become the answer to my prayers too. That's the mystery and beauty of prayer. God doesn't just give us what we ask for; He prepares us to become the very person someone else has been asking Him for.

Friend, whatever insecurity you think disqualifies you from being chosen, God has other plans. As you pray for your future spouse, He is also shaping you through daily faithfulness, integrity, kindness, and trust to become the answer to someone else's prayer.

Heavenly Father, *I thank You that You are the Author of love and the One who hears every prayer. You are faithful to prepare us not only to receive answered prayers but also to become answers to the prayers of others.*

I pray for my future husband today. Shape him into a man of integrity who seeks You first. Teach him to walk in faithfulness and kindness. Grow him into a husband who will enrich my life and bless our future home. Remind him that his waiting is not wasted but part of Your preparation. Help him to be praying for me today as I pray for him.

Would You help me, Lord, that I would also grow in virtue and strength of character so I can be the kind of wife he has prayed for? I pray that in our future marriage, we would be living answers to prayer, fulfilling not only our longings but also the vision You've had for our lives all along. In Jesus' name, amen.

Love in Action . . .

Choose one practical way to live out the qualities of a godly spouse this week, whether it's showing kindness, practicing integrity, or praying with greater consistency as you grow into the answer to someone's prayer.

As I pray for my future spouse, I'm becoming the kind of person they are praying for.

WEEK

45

WHOLENESS IN DESIRE

God's will is for you to be holy, so stay away from all sexual sin. Then each of you will control his own body and live in holiness and honor—not in lustful passion like the pagans who do not know God and his ways.

1 THESSALONIANS 4:3-5

When I was younger, my first experiences with sexuality were tangled with pain and confusion. A classmate crossed boundaries that left me grieving spiritually, even though physically it had felt good. That mix of pleasure and pain left me carrying secrecy and shame, where masturbation became part of my life. Maybe you've been there, too, where desire feels overwhelming or you're unsure how to make sense of it before God.

Here's the good news: Physical desire itself isn't dirty. God designed it as a good gift for marriage, to deepen intimacy and reflect His love. The enemy twists it, however, to enslave us. Scripture calls us to guard our hearts and bodies, to flee lust and impurity (see Matthew 5:28; 1 Corinthians 6:19-20) for our own protection. But even when we struggle, Jesus is able to redeem us and make us whole.

Wholeness begins when we let Jesus meet us in the deeper places of our desires. Sometimes what feels like lust is really loneliness, stress, or old wounds crying out for comfort. Jesus doesn't turn away from those places. He leans in with gentleness. He doesn't just want to end the struggle; He wants to heal the root, restore joy, and bring us into deeper connection with Him.

When desire feels overwhelming, you can redirect it: Pray in the moment, worship, move your body, write, create, or reach out to someone safe. These aren't just distractions; they're ways of shifting your longing toward life and true connection. And if you ever feel stuck in secrecy, remember this: Healing grows in the light. Jesus welcomes you to come as you are, and He walks patiently with you into freedom.

Heavenly Father, *I thank You for being holy, loving, and patient with me. You created desire as a good gift, and You are the One who makes us whole. You are merciful, full of grace, and strong enough to heal every hidden place.*

I pray for my future husband today. Guard his eyes, mind, and heart from lust. Heal him from any past wounds that distort his view of desire. Break every chain of addiction, secrecy, or shame and replace them with purity, joy, and freedom in Christ. Let him find comfort in Your presence, not in counterfeit escapes. Teach him to honor You with his body, his thoughts, and his longings.

Please help me, Lord, that I would also walk in wholeness, surrendering every desire to You and trusting You to make me strong in moments of weakness. Heal places of shame, abuse, and pain in my life. I want my whole life to be surrendered to You. I pray for my future marriage and that our intimacy would be pure, beautiful, and rooted in covenant love, a reflection of Your holiness and a testimony of Your redeeming power. In Jesus' name, amen.

Love in Action . . .

Bring your desires and struggles before Jesus. If you feel caught in lust or addiction, pray for Him to heal the root of your longing. Don't be afraid to invite a trusted counselor, mentor, or friend into the journey. Freedom grows in community, and Jesus delights to meet you there.

Purity isn't perfection; it's about turning daily toward Jesus.

WEEK

PRAYING FOR THE NEXT GENERATION 46

He issued his laws to Jacob; he gave his instructions to Israel. He commanded our ancestors to teach them to their children, so the next generation might know them—even the children not yet born—and they in turn will teach their own children.

PSALM 78:5-6

When you're walking in unmet desires, you might come to a crossroads. You might choose to stay close to others who have what you long for, or you might choose to push them away.

I remember a friend from seminary who was like a sister to me when we were both single. But when Caleb and I started dating, she completely disappeared from my life. Later, she told me she couldn't handle being around anyone who was happily dating or married. That confession explained so much, but it also broke my heart. It reminded me that while it's okay to set boundaries in hard seasons, it's dangerous to close ourselves off from the very relationships God might use to help us grow.

I faced a similar crossroads soon after Caleb and I lost our twins. The pain was crushing, and baby dedications at church were sometimes too much for me. I had to quietly step out, giving myself permission to grieve. But I knew I could not remove myself from others' joy completely or the gifts already present in my life. When my nephews came over to visit, I let myself fully embrace them. I chose to be present at bridal showers for friends, to love the kids in my life, and to keep saying yes to opportunities to invest in the next generation, even while holding space for my own grief.

What I've learned is this: Legacy starts now. You don't have to wait until you're a parent to impact children and younger believers. It can look like being a godparent, praying over nieces and nephews, teaching younger women, or simply opening your life to bless others. Every time Caleb and I get to speak, mentor, or share God's love, we see the fruit of investing beyond ourselves. And I believe this is part of the calling for marriage—not just to bless each other but to leave a spiritual inheritance that ripples into generations to come.

Heavenly Father, *I thank You that You are a God of generations, who is faithful not only to me but to those who will come after me. You weave legacy through love, and You entrust us with opportunities to pass on faith to others.*

I pray for my future husband. Give him a heart that values the next generation. Teach him to love, serve, and mentor children and younger believers with joy. Shape him to be a man who carries blessing into our family line, who prays faithfully for kids we know and even those not yet born. Let him be marked by a vision bigger than himself, with a desire to build a legacy of faith that points others to You.

Please help me also embrace every opportunity You give me to bless and pour into the lives of children and younger believers. I pray for our future marriage, that together we would impact generations, leaving behind a legacy of faith, love, and Christ-centered living that ripples long after we're gone. In Jesus' name, amen.

Love in Action . . .

Ask God to use your future marriage to bless children, nieces, nephews, or younger believers. Write a prayer of legacy for the next generation that He will entrust to you.

My marriage is meant to impact generations to come.

WEEK

47

HEARING GOD'S VOICE IN YOUR LOVE STORY

My sheep listen to my voice;
I know them, and they follow me.
JOHN 10:27

There have been so many seasons in my life when I wanted God to speak with skywriting clarity. I wanted a sign, a dream, a rainbow, anything that would tell me what to do, who to date, where to move, and when my prayers for marriage and family would be answered. Sometimes God has given me a special confirmation, but more often He speaks in quieter, deeper ways: through His Word, His peace, and His gentle no when everything in me wants a yes.

Over time, I have learned something that has changed how I walk with Him: God's goal is not to train us to chase signs but to teach us to know His voice. In my own life, that has looked like moving from "God, give me a sign" to "God, teach me to stay close to You." It has looked like catching myself when I start letting comparison, complaint, or idolatry get loud and instead choosing gratitude, worship, and His truth. It has meant trusting that sometimes He only shows me the next small step instead of the whole plan, and that is still His kindness.

Jesus promises that His sheep hear His voice. That means you are not behind, broken, or "too late" to learn how to walk with Him. The more time you spend in Scripture, the easier it becomes to recognize what sounds like His heart. His voice will never contradict His Word. His leading will not drag you into fear and confusion but will draw you toward peace, repentance, humility, and love.

You do not have to be perfect to hear God. You simply have to be His. As you walk with Him, He knows how to lead you in relationships, timelines, healing, and calling. You may not get a rainbow every time, but you can have something much better every day: the steady, faithful voice of your Shepherd, guiding you one step at a time.

Dear heavenly Father, *thank You that I get the wonderful joy of being Your daughter. You love to communicate with me. Thank You, Jesus, that You are my Good Shepherd and that I am not walking through life alone. Please teach me to know Your voice more clearly through Your Word, Your Spirit, and Your peace.*

I pray for my future husband. May he learn to hear and obey You in the big decisions and in the daily ones. Help him to choose Your voice over the noise of fear, pressure, and comparison.

Prepare us both to be people who follow You even when we do not see the whole plan. When You say "Wait," help us to trust; when You say "Go," help us to obey. Let our future marriage be directed by Your voice above all others. In Your name, Jesus, amen.

Love in Action . . .

Set aside ten to fifteen quiet minutes today with your Bible. Read John 10:1-15 slowly. Underline or highlight every phrase that shows how Jesus cares for and leads His sheep. Then ask Him, “Lord, what is one small step You are inviting me to take today?” Write down what comes to mind. If it matches His character and His Word, choose one way to obey it this week.

His voice brings clarity, not confusion.

Father, thank You that Your timing is perfect and Your ways are higher than mine. You never fail to keep Your promises.

WEEK

48

SEEING MARRIAGE AS A MINISTRY TOGETHER

Go and make disciples of all the nations, baptizing them in the name of the Father and the Son and the Holy Spirit. Teach these new disciples to obey all the commands I have given you.

MATTHEW 28:19-20

Early in our marriage, Caleb and I worked at a Christian school. We had our own classrooms, but the kids knew both spaces were safe. I'll never forget how often we'd visit each other's rooms after school only to find them overflowing with students. They saw our classrooms as a refuge—a place to feel safe, listened to, and cared for.

Some of our students were carrying burdens far bigger than their years. I think of the teenage girl who cried as she told us about her parents' divorce and the boy who opened up about his low self-esteem due to years of not feeling good enough. In those moments, Caleb and I would sit side by side with them, listening, praying over them, and speaking God's love into their lives. Looking back, I can see how powerful it was when Caleb and I came together, not just as two teachers but as a husband-and-wife team, letting God use our marriage as a vessel of His love.

Since those early years, God has expanded the way we serve together—officiating weddings, mentoring couples, speaking at churches, and counseling clients around the world. But the heart of our service hasn't changed. Whether in a classroom, a living room, or halfway across the globe, ministry together means opening our hands and saying, "Lord, use us."

Marriage isn't just about building a home or enjoying life together. It's a mission field. Every time you serve side by side, whether in big or small ways, you're not just strengthening your own bond, you're impacting the Kingdom of God.

Heavenly Father, *I thank You that You invite us into Your mission. You are the God who transforms ordinary moments into eternal impact when we serve in Your name.*

I pray for my future husband. Give him a heart that delights in ministry, whether on big stages or in hidden spaces. Teach him to serve with humility, listen with compassion, and pray with boldness. Shape him into a man who sees our marriage as a partnership for Your Kingdom and longs to multiply Your love wherever we go.

I pray for myself, that I would prepare even now by serving with faithfulness, embracing opportunities to bless others, and letting You shape my heart for ministry. I pray for our future marriage, that when we come together, our love would become a refuge for others, a safe place that reflects Jesus and leaves a legacy that outlasts us. In Jesus' name, amen.

Love in Action . . .

Write down one way you'd love to serve God as a team with your future husband. Pray over it and begin practicing that heart of ministry now on your own.

**Marriage is more than love.
It's ministry together.**

WEEK

49

BELIEVING GOD FOR ABUNDANCE, NOT SCARCITY

The thief's purpose is to steal and kill and destroy. My purpose is to give them a rich and satisfying life.

JOHN 10:10

For years, people told me I was too picky. I heard it so often that fear began to creep in: *Maybe I'm asking for too much. Maybe what I long for in a husband doesn't even exist.* That fear made me settle for relationships that didn't reflect God's best for me. I remember one relationship in particular, where people commented, "He's the best you'll ever get." Deep down, however, the Holy Spirit kept nudging me otherwise.

Walking away felt terrifying. I didn't see Caleb on the other side of that decision. But the moment I obeyed God, I felt peace. It was like a weight lifting from my chest, reminding me that freedom comes when we listen to His voice. Yes, loneliness tried to creep in. Yes, doubts whispered, "What if you made a mistake?" But God's peace kept steadying my heart.

Not long after, Caleb and I began spending time together in groups, and I found myself adoring the little things about him. On our first date, he showed up at my door with chocolate-covered almonds, the very snack I had casually mentioned loving weeks before. That small, thoughtful gesture felt like a God-wink.

With Caleb, I never had to perform or pretend. I could be fully myself, all walls down and heart wide open. For the first time, I felt God's extravagance and abundance. There was no place of fear saying, "Take what you can get." Instead, there was a love story marked by peace and joy I didn't even know was possible.

Friend, scarcity will always tempt you to settle, but peace is the fruit of God's best. His abundance may not come in the way or timing you expect, but when it does, you'll know it was worth the wait.

Heavenly Father, *I praise You as the God of abundance and peace. Thank You that You never call me to settle or measure by the world's standards.*

I pray for my future husband today. Guard his heart from compromise or worldly pressure. Shape his standards to reflect Yours. Teach him to wait on You with courage and joy, knowing You are faithful to provide abundantly.

Please help me to rest in Your peace, even when loneliness or doubt tries to creep in. Anchor me in the truth that Your voice always leads to freedom.

And when You bring us together, Father, may our marriage reflect Your abundance marked by peace, joy, and a love that magnifies You. In Jesus' name, amen.

Love in Action . . .

When the thought *There aren't enough godly men* crosses your mind, replace it immediately with Ephesians 3:20: God is able to do "immeasurably more" (NIV). Speak abundance over your love story.

Scarcity is a lie. God writes stories of abundance.

WEEK

50

PREPARING TO COMMUNICATE WITH GRACE AND TRUTH

Let your conversation be gracious and attractive so that you will have the right response for everyone.

COLOSSIANS 4:6

I've said a million words I wish I could take back. I love Caleb deeply, but sometimes when he says something that brushes against old wounds, I can react with a sharp tone.

If I'm honest, it's not really about him. It's about the internal lie I've carried from my past that says I have to fight for love, fight for respect, and fight for my place. This mindset has me coming out swinging at times, as if every conversation is a battle to win. But the truth is, marriage isn't meant to be a war between you and your spouse. There's one true enemy, and your husband is not it. God never asked me to be my own defender. He's already promised to fight for me (see Exodus 14:14).

The times I've chosen to lay down my sword at Jesus' feet instead of swinging it at Caleb are the moments peace has entered our home. Counseling before marriage gave me the beginning tools, but marriage itself has been the real classroom, teaching me to let God heal my inner dialogue, soften my reactivity, and make me more responsive. I have a long way to go, but I can humbly surrender to Jesus, knowing He will always help me.

I'm so thankful for a husband who gives me grace when I stumble. But here is what I have learned: You don't have to say everything you're thinking. You don't have to fight for your worth. Let God be your defender. Run to Him with your frustration before you unleash it on your spouse. Communication soaked in grace and truth builds connection instead of walls, and it's one of the holiest habits you can begin practicing now.

Heavenly Father, *I thank You for being my defender and my Prince of Peace. You are patient, kind, and full of grace, and You never speak to me harshly. Thank You for teaching me what love sounds like.*

I pray for my future husband today. Guard his tongue and tone with Your Spirit. Teach him to speak with both truth and tenderness, honesty and humility. Protect him from reacting out of anger or fear, and instead, let his words spark life and peace. Surround him with men who model godly communication so that his voice reflects Yours.

Lord, shape me in all the same ways. Heal the places in me that still believe I have to fight for love. Help me pause before I speak, surrendering sharp words to You and choosing responses that honor instead of wound. May our future home be filled with conversations marked by grace and truth. Let our words be a safe place for each other, pointing us back to You and building a love that lasts. In Jesus' name, amen.

Love in Action . . .

Practice this week's verse, Colossians 4:6, by responding to someone in your life with both kindness and honesty. Communication habits you build now will carry into marriage.

Grace and truth together make a strong marriage.

WEEK

51

PRAYING FOR A MARRIAGE THAT LASTS A LIFETIME

Didn't the LORD make you one with your wife? In body and spirit you are his. And what does he want? Godly children from your union. So guard your heart; remain loyal to the wife of your youth.

MALACHI 2:15

It was September, and our mistletoe was still hanging from the last Christmas, a sweet little remnant of the previous year. The flicker of candles lit our living room as rain gently tapped against the windows. All seemed cozy, but my heart was heavy from grief. My grandfather had recently passed away, a friend I loved was going through a hard time, work had been stressful, and Caleb and I weren't in sync. Tension lingered between us as we sat together that night.

But then, under that leftover mistletoe, Caleb reached for me, breaking the tension. We kissed, and he invited me to dance. I let him lead with every spin, and it felt like the tightness in my chest unraveled into peace. The stress melted as I whispered, "Lord, help me follow Your lead by following his. Help this marriage last a lifetime."

That moment reminded me of Jesus' words in Revelation 2 that speak of returning to the love you had at first. When we first fall in love, whether with Jesus or with our spouse, everything feels full of wonder. But over time, the ordinary routine can dull what once made our hearts leap. The secret to a marriage that lasts isn't avoiding the hard seasons. It's choosing to keep going back. To remember how it all began, to see each other with fresh eyes, and to let God awaken the wonder again and again.

That's why I cherish not just the extraordinary moments but the ordinary ones too: enjoying porch dates, having late-night ministry talks, making food side by side, opening our Bibles together, or simply sitting next to each other on the couch. Every single moment I want forever. Even the hard moments I'd take again, as long as I get to walk them with Caleb.

Marriage that lasts a lifetime doesn't happen by accident. It's built choice by choice: to thank God for today, to guard your heart, to remain loyal, and to return to your first love. None of us are promised tomorrow. But today? Today we can cherish the gift of love in our hands and trust God to carry it into forever.

Father, *You are faithful, unchanging, and full of steadfast love. Thank You for showing me what covenant love looks like and for designing marriage to reflect Your heart.*

I pray for my future husband today. Guard his heart with loyalty, faithfulness, and strength. Let him be a man who treasures not just the big milestones but every ordinary moment—someone who will laugh with me in the kitchen, pray with me in the living room, and hold me through the storms. Make him steady, humble, and true.

Teach me to be a wife who cherishes and does not take for granted. Help me to show gratitude in the small things, to extend grace in the hard moments, and to delight in the daily gifts You've placed in front of me.

Lord, would our future marriage not just survive the years to come but flourish in them? May we grow old together with hearts still young in wonder, still loyal in love, and still surrendered to You, the One who makes us one. In Jesus' name, amen.

Love in Action . . .

Write a short prayer asking God to prepare you and your future husband for a covenant that lasts. Keep it in your journal as a reminder of the kind of marriage you're waiting for.

God's design for marriage is faithfulness that lasts a lifetime.

WEEK

52 HOPE THAT NEVER DISAPPOINTS

This hope will not lead to disappointment. For we know how dearly God loves us, because he has given us the Holy Spirit to fill our hearts with his love.

ROMANS 5:5

I've learned something over the years: Caleb is a wonderful husband, but he doesn't make a great god. Anytime I've tried to put him in God's place, the situation crumbles.

There have been moments when we were both so weak, with nothing left to give. Times when I went to Caleb first instead of Jesus, and it set him up to lose. No spouse can carry the weight of being your healer, comforter, or savior. That role belongs to Christ alone.

But when I run to Jesus first, when I invite Him to sit with me in the pain, when I let Him show me where the hurt is coming from, something shifts. My desire is met in Him. My heart is steadied in His love. And only then can I approach Caleb with honesty and tenderness instead of desperation and pain.

Even in the church, people can make marriage sound like the "end prize." But marriage was never meant to be the goal. Jesus is the prize. Marriage is a gift, a reflection, a beautiful cherry on top, but Christ alone is the fulfillment our hearts crave.

If you remember nothing else from these prayers, remember this: Your hope isn't in a husband. Your hope isn't in a marriage. Your hope is in Christ, and that hope will never disappoint.

So keep praying for your future spouse, keep believing in God's best, but never let it become your obsession. Let Jesus stay your first love, and trust Him to give every good gift in His perfect timing. May you step into your future with gratitude and hope, and with your eyes fixed on Christ, the One who never disappoints.

Father, *I thank You for being my first love and the One who never disappoints. You are my comforter, my strength, and the One who fills every empty place with Your perfect love.*

I lift up my future husband to You today. Guard him from the temptation to place his hope in anyone or anything but You. When he is weary, be his rest. When he feels empty, fill him with Your Spirit. Remind him that his worth is not in his performance, or even in our future marriage, but in being Your beloved son. Teach him to draw near to You first so that he can love me from a place of overflowing, not striving.

Lord, help me in all these same ways. Keep me from placing expectations on him that only You can fulfill. Remind me that You are my anchor, my healer, and my joy. Lord, help our future marriage to never become an idol but always be a reflection of You. Let our love be a testimony of Your faithfulness, rooted in the truth that You alone are the prize we live for. In Jesus' name, amen.

Love in Action . . .

Spend five minutes in quiet, thanking Jesus for being your ultimate hope. Remind your heart that marriage is a gift but He alone is your fulfillment.

My hope isn't in marriage. It's in Christ, who never fails.

Acknowledgments

To Jesus, the Savior of my soul. No words can express how You have flipped and keep flipping my life right side up. God, You've held me in the palms of Your hands since I was born. Holy Spirit, You always stay close to me, and I feel Your guidance. Thank You for giving me every good thing and for being the glue in our marriage.

To the love of my life, Caleb. You are the champion of my heart. Sometimes it's easy to take for granted the answered prayers I'm living in every day. Whether it's holding your hand through life, doing ministry with you day in and day out, or writing these books while sitting next to each other on the couch overlooking the beautiful forest, each of these moments is a reminder that God has been so faithful. Being married to you is one of the greatest blessings of my life. You are the joy of my life and the apple of my eye. We've faced so much together in over twelve years of marriage, but I love you even more today than when we began.

Caleb, I still remember in 2014, standing on stage sharing our love story with students. Tears filled my eyes as I thought about the greatness of God, how He redeemed my broken places and gave me you, my walking answer to prayer. And ever since, we've been doing the same: pointing people to His love and remembering that He truly does immeasurably more than we could ever ask, think, or imagine. I love you with all my heart.

To my children, Shiloh and Asher, in heaven. Caleb and I long to hold you in our arms, but we know you are with God. We love you and hope to honor you in how we love and serve others. We can't wait to see you in heaven. To any future children God might bless us with: You will be our redemption story. We love you already.

To my parents, Ed and Susan Stack. You both are my heroes. The older I get, the more I appreciate you both and thank God for you. From the time I was a little girl, you believed in me. You spoke so much encouragement over my creativity in writing and drawing. You have sacrificed so much for me and the dreams God has put on my heart. I'm forever grateful for the love, sacrifice, example, and generosity you have shown me every day of my life. I am so grateful God chose you to be my parents. Your hard-work ethic and the way you pour your heart and soul into loving others is such an inspiration. The way you love and embrace Caleb and have helped our dreams come true is something I cherish always. I love you both so much.

To my in-laws, "Papa" John and "Momma" Kay. Your love for each other, the romance, and the fun you continually cultivate show that love can last forever. Thank you for your support and encouragement in making this dream of ours come true.

Caleb and I feel every prayer, and we are so thankful for all the ways that you are there for us in both the good and difficult times. You motivate us to see the best in each other and to fight for each other in every circumstance.

To my grandma Maryann "Nanny" Miller, my grandpa Bob "Pappy" Miller (now in heaven), and my Aunt Cindy. You are the most generous, loving humans. You continually think of others before yourselves. No matter what you have, you look for ways it can bless others. Pappy wrote me a letter a week for almost ten years. His funny, caring way inspired me to write and go after my dreams. Nanny and Cindy, you continually support and love us and make this world a better place.

To my grandpa Bill Stack, my grandma Tris Stack, and my Aunt Dee (all now in heaven). You continually spoke love and inspiration over me. You've taught me to trust God, and you believed in my ability to write from the time I was little and writing Christmas plays for the family. You cultivated so much fun, joy, and unconditional love. Pappy and Nanny, your love and sacrifice are letting us do dreams now for God's Kingdom that we couldn't do without you. Words can't thank you enough.

To my sister, Cristina. I'm so proud of the amazing woman and mom you are. I'm so grateful for you. It's been a blessing to get to do life together with you since I was two. Thanks for being my little sister and by my side through all the ups and downs. To Daniel, my brother-in-law, and our nephews, Daxton and Kadan: We love you so much. You bring so much joy, laughter, and fun into our lives. I'm so proud of you, Daxton and Kadan. God has such amazing plans for your life! I'm praying already for your future wives!

To Caleb's grandma Marcia. Thank you for your constant and consistent love and words of encouragement. You are an inspiration for endurance and grace in all our lives. You have shown us how to overcome and trust God in every season. We are grateful for you.

To Caleb's brothers, Matt and Jesse. Thanks for being great brothers to Caleb and me! You guys are such a gift. And to Alicia, my sister-in-law, and our niece and nephew, Shirah and Josiah: I am so thankful for each of you, and I appreciate the love and encouragement you always show me. Shirah and Josiah, I'm praying for your future husband and future wife. God has such amazing plans for you!

To my friends, family, and mentors. You are so valued and appreciated. I couldn't have done this project without you. We see you, and we love you so much. Thank you for believing in us. To Chelsea, Nick, Hudson, and Samuel. We love you guys beyond measure. Thanks for being such a faithful friend, Chelsea.

Christy Junod, thank you for loving me so well and fighting for me in prayer and encouragement. Your friendship means the world to me, and we love your family so much!

And to our Bible study family: Brenna, Eileen, Tabitha, David, Justine, Jordan, Molly, Tyler, Dan, Dosalyn, Kelly, and Charles. Your encouragement and prayer have meant more to us than you could know.

To Aunt Nancy, Uncle Danny, and Aaron and Andrew Kohl. To Uncle Ray, Aunt Rebecca, Chris and Kayla Stack, and Sarah and Peter Sheeler. To Uncle Bob, Ryan, Chad, Brandi Radke. Jenni, Gordon, and Isla McMillian. Nikki and Chris

Lee. The Carys. The Rouses. We love our extended family and thank God for each of you.

To my high school best friends Nikki, Lindsay, Lauren, Laura, Amanda, Abby, Jenn, MK, and Megan. Your friendship and support over the years have meant the world to me. I love you all so much.

To my other sisters in Christ whom I love beyond words: Gina, Leanna, Mandy, Jenn, Kirstin, Chelsea, Christina, Greer, Lauren, Tori, Kyra, Sara, Kirby, Wendy, Rory, and all our dear friends. You have each influenced my life in such powerful ways. I'm beyond grateful for each of you.

To Pastors Dave D'Angelo, John Nuzzo, Matt Barnett, and Kurt Bjorklund. We thank God for you being our pastors throughout our walk with God! To our beloved sponsor children, Juan, Samantha, and Victor. We love you and believe in you!

To Sarah Atkinson, Sarah Kelley, and the team at Tyndale House Publishers. Thank you for believing in us, for investing in our dreams, and for helping us share our story with the world. Thank you for your intentional feedback and your kindness, and for crying with us, laughing with us, and pushing us to make this book the best it can be.

To Alex Field and The Bindery Agency. Working with you has allowed us to dream bigger and make a lifelong dream become a reality. We appreciate you for believing in us and for being our advocates throughout this process.

To our Cultivate Relationship, *Wholehearted Love*, and Waiting Well women and men, and to all those we have the huge honor of mentoring. We love you, Laura, Mirta, Michelle, Deanna, Sarah, Kristi, Alisa, Brenda, Makayla, Elisabeth,

Senam, Katarina, Rachel, Hannah, Vienna, Jacquelle, Natalia, Nadine, Chad, Victor, Tobius, and Matthew. And to all the rest, we cherish you. Your courage, love, kindness, and growth are so inspiring. We love you and believe in you. We are so proud of you, and we know God is in the midst of redeeming everything in your life.

To our online community and family all over the world. You are loved beyond measure! God has an amazing plan for your life, and we hope this book inspires you to realize that you are not forgotten. The pain and heartbreak you have experienced are not the end of your story. God has so much in store for you. Thank you for your encouragement and support!

About the Author

Stefanie Rouse and her husband, Caleb, are best friends, partners in life and ministry, and passionate mentors who love walking with singles and couples toward God's best for their relationships. Having experienced both heartbreak and healing in their own journeys, they know firsthand the power of God's redemption in love stories. Their heart is to see others discover the same freedom, hope, and joy that they have found in Christ.

With their master's degrees in education (Caleb) and marriage and family therapy with an emphasis in theology (Stefanie), they combine biblical wisdom, counseling tools, and their own real-life story to encourage people in every stage of their relationships. Together, they lead online communities such as the Waiting Well Singles Community and Cultivate Relationship, where thousands find encouragement, prayer, and practical tools for love that lasts.

As authors of *Wholehearted Love* and the *52 Prayers for My Husband/Wife* series, and as the creators behind @calebjasonrouse, @stefanie.rouse, @ChristianSoulmates, and the *Wholehearted Love*

Podcast, they share daily encouragement with hundreds of thousands around the world. Their vision is simple: to help people love out of the overflow of God's love, creating marriages and families that reflect His goodness.